For Connie and
Denise
a touch of the poet and
a taste of Ireland —
Tim

hiding places

hiding places

Essays

Timothy Brownlow

OOLICHAN BOOKS
LANTZVILLE, BRITISH COLUMBIA, CANADA
2008

Library and Archives Canada Cataloguing in Publication

Brownlow, Timothy
Hiding places : essays / Timothy Brownlow.

ISBN 978-0-88982-251-1

I. Title.

PS8553.R693A16 2008   C814'.54   C2008-903049-4

We gratefully acknowledge the financial support of the Canada
Council for the Arts, the British Columbia Arts Council through
the BC Ministry of Tourism, Small Business and Culture, and the
Government of Canada through the Book Publishing Industry
Development Program, for our publishing activities.

Cover portrait: Michael Warren, 2004

Published by
Oolichan Books
P.O. Box 10, Lantzville
British Columbia, Canada
V0R 2H0
Printed in Canada

In memory of David FitzGerald
colleague, mentor, friend

So feeling comes in aid
Of feeling, and diversity of strength
Attends us, if but once we have been strong.

Oh mystery of man, from what a depth
Proceed thy honours! I am lost, but see
In simple childhood something of the base
On which thy greatness stands—but this I feel,
That from thyself it is that thou must give,
Else never canst receive. The days gone by
Come back upon me from the dawn almost
Of life; the hiding-places of my power
Seem open, I approach, and then they close;
I see by glimpses now, when age comes on
May scarcely see at all; and I would give
While yet we may, as far as words can give,
A substance and a life to what I feel:
I would enshrine the spirit of the past
For future restoration.

William Wordsworth, *The Prelude* (1805), Book Eleventh, 325-342

CONTENTS

1

FAIRIES AND FERRIES

On a recent trip to Ireland, I revisited one of the most famous Joycean shrines: the Martello Tower at Sandycove, County Dublin, where Joyce lived for a very short period with his friend Oliver St John Gogarty. Gogarty was a young poet, wit, and medical student, and he appears as Buck Mulligan in the opening scene of *Ulysses,* shaving on the parapet of the tower and looking down at the "snotgreen, scrotumtightening" sea. The sea at Sandycove, just eight miles outside Dublin, does have an unusual colour, one I have never seen anywhere else, and I used to try to paint it as a boy when I attended the boarding school up the hill. The tower is now a Joyce museum, opened in the summer of 1962. I was one of the guests on that occasion, and remember seeing eminent Joyceans such as Sylvia Beach (who first published *Ulysses* in Paris in 1922) and Anthony Burgess, the novelist, mingling in the crowd.

Apart from its scenic position (there are splendid views of the curve of Dublin Bay, Howth Head, the Wicklow Mountains behind, and the ferries from Wales turning on a sixpence as they swerve into Dun Laoghaire harbour), the tower has many historical associations. It is one of over a dozen of such towers built strategically along the East Coast of Ireland to defend the realm from a possible Napoleonic invasion, and this one was a lookout and arsenal. It now celebrates the explosive talents of one of the towering figures of modern literature, and is complemented on the other side of the country by another tower: Thoor Ballylee in County Galway, now also a museum, where Yeats settled with his wife in a damp old Norman keep (described by Ezra Pound as "Uncle Willie in his tower with the river on the first floor"). The sense of place is a powerful ingredient of Irish literature, and anyone sensitive to the principles of feng shui, that places and buildings have energy flows, can be rewarded with unusually atmospheric visits to these "monuments of unageing intellect."

One of the first exhibits inside the foyer of the Joyce tower is one of Joyce's numerous letters looking for money. The card underneath says drily: "Joyce early developed habits of extravagance that outran his income, and he became an expert borrower." This brings to mind that famous promissory note: one of Joyce's Dublin friends was the poet and mystic George Russell, whose nickname was AE. Joyce, surely deliberately, borrowed money from him, and taking out a slip of paper, scribbled AEIOU. And Sylvia Beach gave as good as she got when she described her Left Bank Paris bookshop, where Joyce was effectively launched and funded, as the Left Bank. Joyce was a relentless and unashamed punster—it was just part of his huge appetite for language. He has been at a great feast of languages and stolen the scraps. Some of my favourite puns include a character in *Ulysses* described as having "poached eyes on ghost", which sounds like an Irish hangover; or the musical string of bird imagery in "nobirdy aviar soar anywing to eagle it." Or Joyce once mentioning to Samuel Beckett that he could "justify" every line of his work.

Or describing his attention to his wife's stories as "evesdropping" (spelled e-v-e). He once said himself, with wicked precision: "Some of my puns are trivial, some quadrivial"; in medieval scholasticism the trivium comprised the three subjects of grammar, rhetoric, and logic; the quadrivium comprised the four subjects of music, astronomy, geometry, and arithmetic. Puns may well be trivial (groan, groan) but may also contain three or four levels of meaning. Reading *Finnegans Wake*, indeed, one feels like a spaced-out Alice in Wonderland trying to navigate a turbulent linguistic ocean. One can only sink or skim.

Joyce is so addicted to plays on words that Stephen Daedalus's famous personal manifesto in *A Portrait of the Artist as a Young Man* could read: " . . . using the only arms I allow myself to use: silence, exile, and [punning]" (Anderson 247). But, of course, this playfulness is only part of his formidable arsenal. To continue the metaphor, he lights what look like innocuous fuses in his early work, which explode in his later work into multiple linguistic fragments. In a famous early poem called "Digging", Seamus Heaney chooses between a spade, a gun, and a pen. Fortunately for posterity, he chose the third option. Similarly, the young Joyce is an Irish revolutionary without a gun; he internalizes the historical violence of Irish history ("history is a nightmare from which I am trying to awake"), takes the English language ("the jinglish janglish"), the language of the conqueror, breaks it into smithereens (lovely Hiberno-English word), then hands it back to the English, as if to say: "There's your language as only an Irishman could write it." One way in which Joyce has been hugely influential on language everywhere is that, now, many brilliant writers from the former colonies are doing the same thing. Just as the Easter Rebellion of 1916 predated all other twentieth-century revolutions (the Russian by just one year), so Joyce and Yeats are among the first literary post-colonials. Whereas Yeats brought off this dangerous feat by, Wilde-like, adopting a mask or many masks, which enabled him to stay in the country, Joyce knew that the spiritual pollution of his country could only be cleansed by a complete break, the break of exile. His splitting of the linguistic atom could only be done in the space-cleared laboratory of his brain, away from the accumulated dust of everyday Dublin life, which he famously defined as "the centre of paralysis." If Yeats went looking for the nearest fairy, Joyce went in search of the nearest ferry. (This punning business is contagious.) "The shortest way to Tara is *via* Holyhead." (Anderson 250). [Tara is the ancient ceremonial site of the high kings of Ireland; Holyhead is the port in North Wales where the Irish ferry docks. So, this sentence means: You become more Irish by leaving Ireland. Or, you find Ireland by abandoning it.]

It is in the conversation with the Dean of Studies, an earnest young English convert to the priesthood, that Joyce adumbrates his unease with the language he has inherited. Stephen has just explained to the Dean that in Drumcondra, a suburb of Dublin, a funnel is called a tundish:

"The language in which we are speaking is his before it is mine. How different are the words *home, Christ, ale, master,* on his lips and on mine! I cannot speak or write these words without unrest of spirit. His language, so familiar and so foreign, will always be for me an acquired speech. I have not made or accepted its words. My voice holds them at bay. My soul frets in the shadow of his language." (Anderson 189)

They are speaking English, of course, Joyce registering that the "priest's voice had a hard jingling tone." (a little fuse lit there to detonate in *Finnegans Wake* as "jinglish janglish"; and remember when Joyce visits Cork with his father, they drive across Cork in a "jingle.") In spite of Daedalus's bravado about his word "tundish", he realizes that for all its colourfulness, the speech of provincial Dublin is archaic (tundish, according to the *OED*, dates from 1388, and was spelled by Shakespeare as two words—"tunne dish"— but is now largely obsolete in standard English). The familiar language of Drumcondra (a dromcondriac appears in the *Wake*) is foreign to the Dean, and modern English is foreign to Daedalus. What is a body to do? Slouch off, like Davin, to learn an ugly, academic version of Gaelic? This, to Daedalus, is just another of those nets flung in the path of the artist or true Irishman trying to escape from the labyrinth of history.

Joyce greatly admired Yeats's work and his work for Ireland (Yeats and Lady Gregory gave generous support to this penniless and arrogant iconoclast), but Joyce held the ideals of the Irish Literary Revival at bay as much as he did standard English. He sensed that if he joined in the recreation of an idealized Celtic past, his work would be side-tracked or derailed. Much of it was indeed "narrow-gauge nationalism", which hardened after independence into a puritanical insularity. It was Yeats's genius that gave it its authenticity and magic, and the discovery of Synge, the flowering of Lady Gregory's multiple talents, and the creation of the Abbey Theatre, among much else, vindicated the inward-turning approach. Joyce turned outward to the "Europe of strange tongues and valleyed and woodbegirt and citadelled and of entrenched and marshalled races." (Anderson 167). We can now see that both directions were converging on the centre and on the central issues, not just for Ireland but also for all readers. As Anthony Burgess once put it: "Ireland, the most fantastic country in the world and perhaps the only one that can be regarded as a custodian of unchanging human truth." And why did Freud say that the Irish were the only people on earth who didn't need psychoanalysis? I suppose because they are at it the whole time and don't need the so-called experts. Or, more likely, as a wag put it, because Dublin is the largest open-air asylum in the world. Anyway, who needs to be freudened when you are trying to be jung at heart?

The final story in *Dubliners*, "The Dead", contains an antagonistic exchange between Miss Ivors, the Gaelic enthusiast, and Gabriel, with whom Joyce must have felt a lot in common:

"O, Mr. Conroy, will you come for an excursion to the Aran Isles this summer?"

[Gabriel explains that he usually goes on a cycling trip in France or Belgium.]

"And haven't you your own language to keep in touch with—Irish?" asked Miss Ivors.

"Well", said Gabriel, "if it comes to that, you know, Irish is not my language."

"And haven't you your own land to visit," continued Miss Ivors, "that you know nothing of, your own people, and your own country?"

"O, to tell you the truth," retorted Gabriel suddenly, "I'm sick of my own country, sick of it!" (Scholes and Litz 188-9)

During the ensuing dance, Miss Ivors leans up to Gabriel's ear and whispers, "West Briton." A West Briton is an Irish person who apes the manners and style of the English, and Gabriel is stung by the insult. Joyce, the narrator, in the background "paring his fingernails," knows that the whole of

Ireland is derivative in this sense—what else could it be after seven hundred and fifty years of colonization? Joyce senses that if he were to stay in Ireland, he might well become either a nationalist prig wearing a circular badge to show his knowledge of Gaelic or Erse (which some Joycean wit later christened the "erse-hole of Ireland"), or become an ineffectual aesthete like Gabriel. The story ends famously with the whole of Ireland covered in a blanket of snow. There is even a little cap of snow on the top of the Wellington Monument in Phoenix Park, that tribute to the Anglo-Irishman who settled affairs with Napoleon, making the Martello Towers obsolete. And need I mention the hay Joyce makes elsewhere out of a park named Phoenix, knowing full well that it got its name, not from classical sources but from the Gaelic name for the weir near by, *fionn uisce*, white water? Joyce puts the Ivors/Gabriel debate on ice, as it were, while he gets on with the huge task of dissolving these tensions in his imagination.

It must be admitted that the portrait of his early self that emerges from *A Portrait of the Artist as a Young Man* (published in 1916 after ten years' gestation and revision) is not entirely a flattering one. Joyce once said to a friend: "I've been rather hard on that young man." But it is, of course, a fictional portrait and can be read from many angles. Joyce himself undercuts this previous book in his third book, *Ulysses*, published on his fortieth birthday in 1922:

"Reading two pages apiece of seven books every night, eh? I was young. You bowed to yourself in the mirror, stepping forward to applause earnestly, striking face. Hurray for the Goddamned idiot! Hray! No-one saw: tell no-one. Books you were going to write with letters for titles. Have you read his F? O yes, but I prefer Q. Yes, but W is wonderful. O yes.

W. Remember your epiphanies written on green oval leaves, deeply deep, copies to be sent if you died to all the great libraries of the world, including Alexandria? Someone was to read them there after a few thousand years, a mahamanvantara. Pico della Mirandola like. Ay, very like a whale. When one reads these strange pages of one long gone one feels that one is at one with one who once." (3. 136-46)

This cheerful self-mockery is given a grimly sardonic twist by Joyce's disciple and amanuensis, Samuel Beckett, in *Krapp's Last Tape*:

"Just been listening to that stupid bastard I took myself for thirty years ago, hard to believe I was ever as bad as that. Thank God that's all done with anyway . . . Seventeen copies sold, of which eleven at trade price to free circulating libraries beyond the seas. Getting known . . . Crawled out once or twice, before the summer was cold. Sat shivering in the park, drowned in dreams and burning to be gone." (Harrington 317)

I have already alluded to Hiberno-English. This is the term for the hybrid language, still spoken and written in Ireland today, resulting from the historical collision between Standard English and Gaelic. As the Irish were more and more compelled, by education and economic necessity, to cast off the rags of Gaelic and don the more respectable, and profitable, cloak of English, they cut the cloth of their speech in an idiosyncratic way by keeping much of the syntax of Gaelic along with many archaisms in the conqueror's tongue. We have seen "tundish" as an example. A courtliness of speech and manner at all levels of society was much noticed by visitors to Ireland until recently, and writers such as Synge fell in love with it. But where Synge exploits the extravagance of that language ("It's that you'd say surely and you seen him, and he after drinking for weeks, rising up in the red dawn or before it maybe . . ."), Joyce in his early work pares down the language to an exhilarating clarity. The older I get, the more I re-joyce in the way scenes and images from Joyce's writing have stuck in my mind for decades: one example from *A Portrait of the Artist as a Young Man* is the miraculously simple description of the way a napkin ring rolls across the table and comes to rest at the foot of an easy chair just as Aunt Dante violently leaves the dinner table, delivers herself of the "very bad language" of religious passion, and slams out of the room. No wonder Beckett was a devotee of Joyce. Beckett strips language back even further.

Another lasting image is the etched impression of snow on the spiked gate at the end of "The Dead":

"Yes, the newspapers were right: snow was general all over Ireland. It was falling on every part of the dark central plain, on the treeless hills, falling softly upon the Bog of Allen and, farther westward, softly falling into the dark mutinous Shannon waves. It was falling, too, upon every part of the lonely churchyard on the hill where Michael Furey lay buried. It lay thickly drifted on the crooked crosses and headstones, on the spears of the little gate, on the barren thorns." (Scoles and Litz 223-4)

And then there is the way the stout bottles, warmed before the fire, go "Pok" in "Ivy Day in the Committee Room." Or the way Little Chandler's fingernails describe perfect half-moons in the story "A Little Cloud." Joyce describes his method in *Dubliners* as one of "scrupulous meanness"; paradoxically, the effect is one of a generous increase in vividness.

This vividness owes a lot to the oral tradition. Many Irish people are all talk and no action, like Joyce's father, or, more spectacularly, Oscar Wilde (who elevated dandyism, or studied idleness, into a radical programme for social reform). *A Portrait of the Artist as a Young Man*, is, among other things, an exorcising by Joyce of his father's charming fecklessness. The schoolboy Daedalus describes his father as a "gentleman". Later, there is a chillier description:

"A medical student, an oarsman, a tenor, an amateur actor, a shouting politician, a small landlord, a small investor, a drinker, a good fellow, a storyteller, somebody's secretary, something in a distillery, a taxgatherer, a bankrupt and at present a praiser of his own past." (Anderson 241)

The weak, feckless, abusive, or absent father is a leitmotif of modern Irish literature. George Bernard Shaw once asked his mother: "Is Father drunk?" receiving the exasperated reply: "Is he ever anything else?" This sense of sinking family fortunes prompted Shaw to later describe himself as a "downstart." Yeats's father, a brilliant painter, was another charmer who once said to W. B. after the almost starving young poet had failed to get a job: "You have taken a great weight off my mind." The elder Yeats was incapable of finishing his canvases, with the result that he rarely got paid. The men in O'Casey's plays are hopeless dreamers, leaving the women to do the heroic work of a disintegrating world. Synge's Playboy strikes his da on the head with a spade in an attempt to rid himself of tyranny. Joyce's early years were spent in a demoralizing atmosphere of moving from one shabby dwelling to another, even shabbier one. Joyce's rejection of Faith, Family, and Fatherland is therefore an act of survival as he rejects God the Father, John Joyce the father, and Mother Ireland. He has to father and mother himself into existence as an artist in the vacuum left by this clear cutting. *A Portrait of the Artist as a Young Man* opens with a real father telling his son a story about a moocow; in the diary at the end of the book, the narration changes from third-person to first-person, and the father at its conclusion has become a mythical one, the craftsman Daedalus: "Old father, old artificer, stand me now and ever in good stead." (Anderson 253). The only thing that John Joyce can stand is a drink. Which reminds me of Wilde's (or his character Jack's) description of Lady Bracknell in *The Importance of Being Earnest*: ". . .she is a monster, without being a myth, which is rather unfair." Joyce's father was not a monster, but by converting him into a myth, Joyce is beginning to see his way out of the labyrinth of the family, described by Shaw as *Heartbreak House*. This accounts for the seeming callousness in Stephen Daedalus: like many an Irish exile, he has to reject what he really loves. He is a prodigal son lamenting an equally prodigal father.

But there is an enigma here. Joyce is stylistically in tune with his iconoclastic contemporaries, who had the gargantuan task of dragging art, literature, science, and philosophy into the twentieth century. One thinks of such figures as T. S. Eliot, Ezra Pound, Marcel Proust, Virginia Woolf, Picasso, Braque, Stravinsky, Freud, Jung, and Einstein. Many of these pioneers have the ruthlessness of all revolutionaries. Joyce, however, for all his rejection of Faith, Family, Fatherland, is still, content-wise, unrepentantly old-fashioned. This, like his genius for repetition without overdoing it, is part of his debt to the oral tradition. He is as much an "earwitness" as an eyewitness. As one recent critic has wisely pointed out, Joyce, for all his demolition work, maintains an affection for the middle range of human experience, which makes him, in the words of Christopher Butler, "the most

humorous and charitable of all twentieth-century writers."
(Attridge 279). If, in Marxist terminology, he excoriates the
"bourgeois," Joyce has a devotion to ordinary experience,
bourgeois included, which has endeared him to millions.
(I have already mentioned the Irish resistance to Freud; it is
worth mentioning also that intellectual Marxism has never taken root in Ireland). Joyce once remarked to Arthur
Power that "idealism is the ruin of man" (Attridge 260). I
think he had in mind the extremities to which some abstract
philosophies and ideologies can go (there is a chilling moment in the movie about the capture of Adolf Eichmann
when Eichmann, the engineer of mass murder, calls himself
an idealist.) Joyce's realism is searching but charitable. He
shares this characteristic with his great Irish contemporary,
Yeats, who could certainly take flights into the dim inane,
but who comes to roost in "the foul rag-and-bone shop of
the heart."

Joyce, then, rebels against Mother Church, but uses religious terminology throughout his work. He rebels against
his mother and father, but remains himself a devoted family man. He rebels against Mother Ireland, but remains in-
tensely Irish. He once compared his craft to the work of the
scribes who created great medieval Celtic manuscripts such
as *The Book of Kells*—there is the same circularity, interlocking patterns, obsessive detail, and, above all, conviction. The
gospel according to Joyce is an illuminated manuscript designed by a radically skeptical mind, but one in touch with
ancient mysteries. Joyce also compared his work to a Gothic
Cathedral, specifically Notre Dame de Paris. Having escaped
from various forms of mothering, he wrote his greatest work
within reach of the "everlasting arms" of Our Lady of Paris,
built during the great thaw of the twelfth century.

If Joyce's writings were the threads that led him safely out of the Cretan/Irish labyrinth, and the "lapwing poet" was able to fly by the ensnaring nets, losing Icarus on the way, maybe in another interpretation, he never escaped the maze, but reached the man-eating monster at the centre, slew it, and made the place habitable for the human imagination. Classical labyrinths were often a symbolic quest for the Centre, a Paradise contained and regained. Having escaped the nets of his youth, Joyce creates a linguistic internet, moving from the Sandycove tower to a veritable postmodern Tower of Babel. He left the nowhere of provincial Dublin, and wrote it up as an everywhere.

About to leave Ireland for the first time in 1902, this priest of the eternal imagination wrote to Lady Gregory, who had sent him money and offers of friendship. Lady Gregory, who knew at close quarters the steely vapourings of another friend she suspected of being a genius (W. B. Yeats), probably had mixed feelings as she read this letter (Joyce was only twenty in 1902): maternal solicitude for a willful Icarus taking off with ill-prepared wings, yet with a mumbled hoorah for yet another Irish writer taking on the world (did she not write of the Irish as having "an incorrigible genius for myth-making"?) This time, she was on to another winner. Here is the letter:

"I shall try myself against the powers of the world. All things are inconstant except the faith of the soul, which changes all things and fills their inconstancy with light. And though I seem to have been driven out of my country here as a misbeliever I have found no man yet with a faith like mine." (Anderson 550)

Joyce got on to that ferry, took the Irish Mail train to Euston Street Station in London, and was met at six in the morning by Yeats with offers of breakfast, help, and influential contacts (Foster 275-8). Modern literature has never looked back.

2

THE NAMING OF PARTS

What's in a name? Everything. At least in one's imagination. The names of places, people, families, institutions, houses, have always echoed in my mind. Bill Bryson, in his book about Britain—*Notes from a Small Island*—has only the tip of his tongue in his cheek when he writes: "I genuinely believe that one of the reasons Britain is such a steady and gracious place is the calming influence of the football results and shipping forecasts." (139) Bryson is referring to the old BBC weather forecast, its list of coastal regions around the British Isles reminiscent for Seamus Heaney of "Sirens of the tundra,/Of eel-road, seal-road, keel-road, whale-road . . ." (*New Selected Poems* 115).

Those rhythms summon up my boyhood: afternoon tea at winter dusk with my mother in the sitting-room of our farmhouse, Ballanagh House, between Avoca and Arklow, with its big bay window sprinkled with raindrops. The lamps were subdued, allowing the sputtering coal-fire to throw jumpy shadows on walls and ceiling. After one of my mother's favourite radio programmes—*Animal, Vegetable, or Mineral?* or *Mrs. Dale's Diary*—would come the weather forecast, often with gale warnings, making one shiver with gratitude that one was dry, well-fed, and cosy: "Viking rising five, backing four; Dogger blowing strong, steady as she goes; Minches gale force twelve; Rockall . . . ."

The forecast had the effect of an incantation, of not only focusing the attention but also of propelling the imagination into unexplored regions of thought and feeling, akin to the brain-altering sounds of great music or poetry. Outside, a wind was getting up, casting leaves on the sloping lawn, swaying the upper branches of the huge beech-trees, stirring the old rhododendrons. From the smaller window above the wireless cabinet, beyond the privet hedge moist with rain, the stable door swayed, the fir-trees were agitated. Mauve-ochre clouds piled up over the interlocking lines of the Wicklow hills. The gutters of the house started to chatter.

Bryson mentions the recitation of soccer teams. My equivalent from radio of the fifties was the soothing voice of John Arlott, who was a policeman when "discovered" by John Betjeman, another radio natural. Arlott could give the most banal action on the cricket field an aura of artistic contemplation: "Here at the Oval, just ten minutes to lunch-time, there is a slight drizzle and an easterly breeze, making it a bowlers' wicket. And Laker comes up to bowl from the Pavilion End, a googly—Richie Benaud shapes up to play it, —HE'S GONE—leg before wicket, an unplayable ball—now Australia are 127 for six, and will need 245 runs to force a draw—Keith Miller is their man, and here he is coming out from the Pavilion . . ." all in a rich Somersetshire accent, tangy as cider.

I also share Bryson's love of place-names. Travelling is greatly enhanced by allowing place-names to work their magic. This, of course, goes far beyond the aesthetic: place-names are time-capsules capable of releasing their compressed histories. In Ireland, there is a constant cross-hatching between the original Gaelic names and their translated equivalents. One may deplore the loss of original associations and ways of life, but often the usurping name has acquired its own rich loam. In any long-settled area, this process happens all the time. The Englished name often retains the original meaning: Glendalough is recognisably "Glen of the Two Lakes". Other translations sound made up, but a town such as Ballydehob is not a fictional invention, as is Ballykissangel (Avoca) in the TV series. English names are an amalgam of Celtic, Roman, Norse, Norman and other influences. Take any ten square miles of a map of England, and you'll find riches galore: Buckland-Tout-Saints; Hutton-Le-Hole; Shipton-Under-Wychwood; Britwell Salome; Kingston Bagpuize; Nether Wallop.

Just as listening to the radio exercises the imagination, travelling by train allows the mind's eye to roam in a detached way. This is beautifully caught by Edward Thomas in his poem "Adlestrop," in which the poet remembers a day in June when the train stopped briefly at an out-of-the way station:

> The steam hissed. Someone cleared his throat.
> No one left and no one came
> On the bare platform. What I saw
> Was Adlestrop—only the name . . .

This timeless moment when nothing happens except a pause in a journey attunes his ear, and his imagination is suddenly and marvellously extended:

And for that minute a blackbird sang
Close by, and round him, mistier,
Farther and farther, all the birds
Of Oxfordshire and Gloucestershire.
(*Collected Poems* 25)

The resonance of that moment is similar to that evoked by
Ted Hughes in describing a moat with pike in it: "Stilled
legendary depth:/It was as deep as England." (Geddes 374)

Railway stations are romantic in a way that airports never are.
What a thrill for a boy as the Irish mail train—usually after a
rough mailboat crossing and a fitful sleep in an overcrowded
compartment—slowly squealed its way between moss-cov-
ered walls into Euston Station with dozens of London tax-
ies waiting, their diesels rattling. You go to Paddington for
the West Country, Waterloo for the Continent (now via the
Chunnel), Saint Pancras (whose neo-Gothic atmosphere is
worth the price of a rail ticket) for the non-stop train to
Cambridge, Liverpool Street for the one to Cambridge that
stops about twenty-three times at places like Audley End.
Trans-continental trains, whether the Orient Express (Paris,
Venice, Trieste, Istanbul . . .), Russian, or Canadian are especially evocative. What child is not intrigued by Medicine
Hat and Moose Jaw? I know someone who made a special
trip to Saskatoon, because the ring of "Saskatoon, Saskatch-
ewan" had enchanted him since boyhood. I remember, in
my early days in Canada, standing in the old Union Station
in Toronto and allowing the huge map of Canada to unfold
as the English names of cities were called out, followed by
the French version—ending with a flourish: "CALGAREE
et VAWNCOUVEHR."

The names of houses are especially evocative. One may have

28

to live in a succession of dozens of places, whose postal addresses may be bland and anonymous, but their names as used by the inhabitants are part of one's mental landscape: "Do you remember that day at Ballanagh when the pig got into the sitting-room? Or the day you were chased by a bull in the grounds of Shelton Abbey? Remember the view of the Lakes from Aghadoe? Or the vista of Dublin Bay from Ceanchor Cottage? Or Mrs Maxwell summoning her staff with a whistle at Roxboro? Or the lawn-tennis parties at The Needles, often called off because of Irish rain? Or the deep blue of the rhododendrons at Ballyarthur? The line of purplish hills from the porch at Munny House? Remember the au pair's lover scaling the steep roofs of the Old Glebe? That lovely spring wedding, with the arch of daffodils around the door, at The Moat? Playing among the haycocks at Edenderry?"

One of my oldest friends has lived all his life at a house called Vallombrosa. I was once travelling through the hills near Siena when I came upon the little town of Vallombrosa, from where I sent a post card to Vallombrosa. Nestled along the banks of the Dargle, its lofty beeches giving intermittent glimpses of the perfect profile of the Big Sugar Loaf mountain, the property lives up to its source in *Paradise Lost*:

> Thick as autumnal leaves that strow the brooks
> In Vallombrosa, where th'Etrurian shades
> High overarched imbower.

Many such places, if they are seemingly unspoiled by modernity, are called idyllic; the name acts as a thread of continuity through the maze of change and decay. In a manner reminiscent of Chekhov's *The Cherry Orchard*, the apple orchard at Vallombrosa has given way to a dual-carriage highway, providing relentless background noise. But the name will always stir my five senses: memories of shifting light on the slopes of the Sugar Loaf; the spill of grandfather-clock chimes down the hall staircase; the scent of verbena after rain outside the front door; the chill of autumn winds on the cheek as the beech trees "strew" their leaves in the "shady vale" of the Dargle; a long walk in the Wicklow Hills, followed by turkey stock soup in the tiled country kitchen.

The old-fashioned boarding school was an echoing-chamber of names, mostly incomprehensible outside its walls. Not only were buildings named, but also classrooms: Singleton, Stafford-O'Brien, Beresford. During an early stint of school-mastering, I lived in the Cadogan Building, one of whose entrances was a dark, dank, twisty corridor called the Khyber Pass. Coming back late at night to my room, I was likely to be ambushed by rats—in fact, a parent was once coming to see me when she trod on a rat. The Cadogan Building has recently been refurbished, and is now the musical centre of the college. Directly under my former room, the builders found old cellars that had been closed off. If only I had known—the rats obviously did.

Schoolboys (this was a decade before the place became co-educational) have a genius for nicknames: Mr. Kelly became Spiddo; Mr. Mills was Hut the Miller; the Warden was Hank (as in the Latin *hic, hanc, hoc*); and a young master with a jerky walk and a prominent neck-bone was Turkey. One good-looking older boy was nicknamed Vision; in chapel, when the assembled boys were singing the lovely old Irish hymn, "Be Thou My Vision," everyone turned to look at him. I would like to think that the generality of boys remembered my witticisms and endearing eccentricities: however, most of them if asked forty years later will hoot with laughter and remember Trog—as in Troglodyte, a denizen of dark caves. Perhaps anyone who had to enter his room through the Khyber Pass could only be a primitive. It is nice to know that, in ornithology, wrens—my favourite birds—are known as troglodytes because they build their nests in holes. It is also good to remember that as a boy at the same school, I was known by the happier name of Danny, because my elder brother's nickname was Dan. When I meet contemporaries and pupils from that era, I don't know what to call them, only knowing either their formal school name, as in Jones minor, or their nickname, as in Snowball (whose cousins were known as Snowflake and Snowdrop). Nobody was ever called by his Christian name.

Mention of chapel services at school reminds me of the pleasure I used to get singing in the choir. This was both a musical and a linguistic education. Most boys would groan inwardly when Psalm 104 was announced, but I relished every one of its thirty-six verses, so great was the anticipated relish of singing the word "Leviathan" in verse twenty-six: "There go the ships: and there is that Leviathan whom thou hast made to take his pastime therein." This one exotic word sets off the whole like a diamond, and is followed by the wonderfully deadpan word "pastime." Many writers up to recent times have acknowledged the inspiration drawn in their mature years from the imagery and rhythms of great religious texts, which entered their minds almost unconsciously from a young age.

As a student, I was living in Bordeaux one summer, and was asked by a friend to drive him around as he tasted wines. He was training for the wine trade under the auspices of a large New York wine house, so his card opened all doors. To this day, I cannot study a map of that region of France without

31

a huge nostalgia for the impulses of youth and the remembered power of those French names of regions and chateaux to evoke a world of intrigue and enchantment: Pomerol, Haut-Brion, Margaux, Lafite-Rothschild, Saint Emilion, Pauillac, Drucu-Beaucaillou, Pétrus, and the greatest white wine of them all—D'Yquem.

In one of the videos in which the actors of the Royal Shakespeare Company rehearse Shakespeare, there is a spoof scene in which an actor forgets his lines, those listing the titles of the French nobility in *Henry V*. He very sensibly substitutes made-up titles concocted from memories of half-forgotten meals: Le Duc de Margaux, Le Baron Châteauneuf-du-Pape, Le Marquis de Saint-Emilion, Le Prince D'Yquem, and so on. The joke points up the fascination all writers have with names, which are potent clues to the character of a place, region, or country.

What would England be without the ceremony of Swan Upping on the Thames? Or the guild that calls itself The Worshipful Company of Goldsmiths, or all those pub signs whetting one's thirst with Eagle and Child and Crown and Anchor? My favourite is Ye Olde Trip to Jerusalem (probably England's oldest pub). Oxford and Cambridge colleges, many of them famously in the vanguard of learning, have little survivals that enchant: the toast after dinner at one college: "I give you the Queen"; the ceremony at King's College, Cambridge, in which the Provost walks up the aisle holding a single red rose—the red rose of Lancaster. And I was once passing the Porter's Lodge at Jesus College, Cambridge when the porter answered a ringing phone: "Jesus here." And what about Cockney rhyming slang? Instead of saying "I'll take a look", a Cockney will say: "I'll take a butcher's" (because "butcher's hook" rhymes with "look").

A "door" is a "Rory O'More." Who can resist a book on organic gardening by one Bob Flowerdew? I can't. And who wouldn't want legal counsel from a firm called Argue and Phibbs—a former Dublin establishment?

Then there is the music of names: "Saint Endellion! Saint Endellion!" wrote John Betjeman, "The name is like a ring of bells" (Guest 147). And what about Clunton, Clunbury, Clungunford, and Clun in Shropshire, in whose syllables reverberate tones as mellow and ancient as the medieval bells in nearby belfries? Those writing in the English language have a rich quarry to mine; as great writers demonstrate, the language has an ability to deconstruct and refurbish itself from within, as it were. No one knew this more than Joyce, whose mental radio was tuned into linguistic frequencies on multiple channels: "Teems of times and happy returns . . . . Anna was, Livia is, Plurabelle's to be . . . . Latin me that, my trinity scholard . . . . I feel as old as yonder elm. A tale told of Shaun or Shem? All Livia's daughter-sons . . . . I feel as heavy as yonder stone. Tell me of John or Shaun? Who were Shem and Shaun the living sons or daughters of? Night now!"

Names echo down the centuries, as sturdy and weather-beaten as old buildings, even if the brambles grow inside them and the rooks wheel around their gables: Fountains, Tintern, Glendalough, Clonmacnoise, Loch Leven, Glastonbury . . .

What's in a name? Everything.

3

ACQUIRING A SECOND SKIN

In his amusing and scurrilous reminiscences of the Irish Literary Revival—*Hail and Farewell*—George Moore makes numerous digs at Yeats's behaviour and bohemian apparel: Yeats is described, among other things, as looking like an umbrella left behind after a picnic party and like a Bible preacher. But Moore laces his outrageous and loose-flowing narrative with some acute comments. He is constantly struck by the contrast between Yeats's fascinating presence, especially his captivating talk, and the relative immaturity of his early work. Yeats, like the youthful Wordsworth, seems to have given onlookers an impression of potential genius, though in each case, just what shape that genius might take was problematic. Moore writes that Yeats in the flesh was more intelligent than his verse had led [him] to believe, and that his conversation had a flavour, although too mystical for Moore's taste, that his work could not match: "Yeats is thinner in his writings than in his talk; very little of himself goes into his literature—very little can get into it, owing to the restrictions of his style." (*Ave* 47)

In poetic terms, Yeats was what is called a late developer. This is not to deny the seductive beauty of much of his early verse, but to corroborate Moore's insight that the young poet had created a fine sieve through which only rarified materials could filter. The progress of his career is a gradual expansion of expressive powers, so eventually he is able to throw almost anything into his verse. Yeats himself was aware of this problem; he later wrote that at that time he was striving to move from the poetry of "longing and complaint" towards the poetry of "insight and knowledge." He perceptively writes of Synge's early work, in a phrase that echoes Moore's about his own work, that "life had cast no light into his writings" (*Essays and Introductions* 298). At the time Moore first met him, Yeats was too preoccupied with Celtic Twilight to pay much attention to the light of common day. If Yeats had died, say, in 1912—even with the edition of his *Collected Works* already under his belt—he would probably be known today as an interesting but minor poet. The Easter Rebellion of 1916, just as it changed Ireland for ever, changed Yeats for ever. From then on, stops on his instrument that had lain unused were pulled out, until by the late 1920s the Yeatsian music was performing at full organ. Other factors in this maturation process were his fruitful literary friendship with Ezra Pound, and his delighted discovery that his wife, whom he married in 1917, had remarkable psychic powers.

In his elegy for Lady Gregory's son, "In Memory of Major Robert Gregory", Yeats compares two kinds of achievement:

> Some burn damp faggots, others may consume
> The entire combustible world in one small room
> As though dried straw, and if we turn about
> The bare chimney is gone black out
> Because the work had finished in that flare.
> (Finneran 134-5)

Robert Gregory's talents were combustible, while Yeats's were of the smouldering kind, creating a lot of smoke until the damp faggots dried out. Yeats's early behaviour, as maliciously satirised by Moore, was a smoke-screen to protect his slow-moving talent from the more facile chatterboxes such as Moore. Yeats gave as good as he got, later describing Moore as "a man carved out of a turnip, looking out of astonished eyes." (*Autobiographies* 405)

Yeats's lasting strength arises from his constant awareness of the nature of his talent. He is sometimes ridiculed for his obsession with the occult and his dabblings in magic practices; this, however, seems to have been all part of the smouldering process and one that indeed paid rich dividends. In one of a series of literary clerihews, I emphasize this aspect of his development:

> W. B. Yeats
> Is with the greats.
> With what seems hocus-pocus
> He got his lines in focus.

Moore laughs at the hocus-pocus, but he had no monopoly on catty anecdotes. Yeats wrote of Moore: "All his friends suffered in some way; good behaviour was no protection, for it was all chance whether the facts he pursued were in actual life or in some story that amused him." And Yeats recounts how one evening, he was walking in a narrow street in London, and "heard a voice resounding as if in a funnel, someone in a hansom cab was denouncing its driver, and Moore drove by." (*Autobiographies* 403)

Another metaphor for the gradual development of technique is cogently expressed by the critic M. L. Rosenthal in *Running to Paradise: Yeats's Poetic Art*:

"[Yeats's] technical skill grew like a second skin, enabling him at last to write brilliantly within and around the limits of traditional metrics. He taught himself to use conventional verse so naturally, with such supple variety, that in his hands it almost became a rare, highly disciplined species of free verse." (xiv)

This second skin takes many years to acquire. In the acquisition of poetic technique Yeats takes, as it were, the ready-made clothes from the rack of tradition and tries them on in front of "mirror after mirror" until they acquire the shape of his body. And the celebrated gift of the gab that Moore admires comes into play, as Yeats was always ambitious to give formal utterance the sound of the speaking voice. He had been astonished in his youth by such abrasively brilliant speakers as J. F. Taylor, and he had heard Wilde expound his aesthetic theories in flawless cadences. Yeats set himself consciously to make his own hesitant utterances more effective. John Butler Yeats was a crucial influence here, too, as his conversational sallies were famous.

Yeats turned fifty in 1915, but it is only in his middle and late middle age that this arduous apprenticeship really begins to pay off. The poem on Robert Gregory demonstrates the new spare, colloquial style, as if he were poetically nodding to what he praises in Gregory's art: "To that stern colour and that delicate line/That are our secret discipline/ Wherein the gazing heart doubles her might." (Finneran 134). Another aspect of this hard-won style is, paradoxically, its common humanity, a quality Yeats shares with his great Irish contemporary, Joyce. Denis Donoghue comments :

"A good deal of the brilliant literature of our time has been unfair to Man's potentialities . . . [it] takes little or no account of that great middle range of experience which is still the occasion of generous feeling in many thousands of people. When we think of the common life and of the values which often sustain it, very often we think of it in Yeats's terms." (Donoghue 16-17)

One of the characteristics of this generous feeling is the ability and willingness to praise, a virtue seemingly gone out of fashion in life and literature. Yet praise is as central to Yeats's work as it is to his actions: one thinks of his defence of Synge, his loyalty to friends, and, above all, his appreciations of Lady Gregory. One still finds Yeats occasionally referred to as a snob, as in a recent *Irish Times* article about the current Yeats exhibition at the National Library. Yeats could make silly remarks, picked up again by the remorseless George Moore, but it is a strange kind of snob who can write the following:

"It is hardly an exaggeration to say that the spiritual history of the world has been the history of conquered races. Those learned in the traditions of many lands, understand that it is almost always some defeated or perhaps dwindling tribe hidden among the hills or in the forests, that is most famous for the understanding of charms and the reading of dreams, and the seeing of visions." (*Uncollected Prose* vol. 2, 70)

Bound up with Yeats's love of Ireland is his awareness of its spiritual distinction in the teeth of centuries of political and cultural setbacks, and his praise of Synge and Lady Gregory is of a piece with this love of lost causes, as he was more aware than most of their tragic destiny and that of their ilk. Poetry, for Yeats, to paraphrase his beloved Blake, builds mansions in the ruins of time. And he prophesied the ruin of Lady Gregory's own house in "Coole Park, 1929":

I meditate upon a swallow's flight,
Upon an aged woman and her house,
A sycamore and lime-tree lost in night
Although that western cloud is luminous,
Great works constructed there in nature's spite
For scholars and for poets after us,
Thoughts long knitted into a single thought,
A dance-like glory that those walls begot.

There Hyde before he had beaten into prose
That noble blade the Muses buckled on,
There one that ruffled in a manly pose
For all his timid heart, there that slow man,
That meditative man, John Synge, and those
Impetuous men, Shawe-Taylor and Hugh Lane,
Found pride established in humility,
A scene well set and excellent company.

They came like swallows and like swallows went,
And yet a woman's powerful character
Could keep a swallow to its first intent;
And half a dozen in formation there,
That seemed to whirl upon a compass point,
Found certainty upon the dreaming air,
The intellectual sweetness of those lines
That cut through time or cross it withershins.

Here, traveller, scholar, poet, take your stand
When all those rooms and passages are gone,
When nettles wave upon a shapeless mound
And saplings root among the broken stone,
And dedicate—eyes bent upon the ground,
Back turned upon the brightness of the sun
And all the sensuality of the shade—
A moment's memory to that laurelled head.
(Finneran 242-3)

This poem combines praise, the common touch, and the plangent stateliness of his later work. It has acquired many skins; it crams a lifetime of experience, disappointment, and achievement into four stanzas. That luminous West of Ireland evening light blends with a penetrating intellectual light to suffuse the poem with its elegiac glow. I have several times obeyed the injunction at the end of the poem, turned my back upon the brightness of the sun, and stood at Coole quietly thanking Lady Gregory for her achievement. The house has gone, but on the site there is greensward surrounding the passages of the original foundation. In the turbulent 1920s, when many a landlord's house was burned down, Coole remained untouched. This wasn't just chance; Lady Gregory was not only a famous author and director of the Abbey Theatre, but also the author of a series of articles in *The Times* (London) condemning the cruelties of the Black and Tans in her own locality. In the following four lines, "Coole Revisited," I attempt to catch my belief that Coole is the *fons et origo* of much of subsequent Irish cultural achievement:

Not a blackened burnt-out shell,
Just foundations in good repair:

Foundation of much that bodes well,
Lost rooms a honeycomb in air.

Jon Stallworthy, in *Between the Lines* (Oxford 1963) remarks
that "Few readers of ["Coole Park, 1929"] would guess
that behind its comparatively simple structure and fluent
rhythms lie thirty-eight pages of working—more than went
to the making of any other poem that I know" (200). If
we work backwards from the finished poem, we can peel
several skins from the text until we arrive at the initial prose
version, quoted by Stallworthy. Yeats's mastery is revealed
by the enormous distance travelled, the alchemical process
achieved, from halting notations to singing lines. The germ
of the poem is expressed in the prose draft:

"Describe house in first stanza. Here Synge came, Hugh
Lane, Shaw Taylor, many names. I too in my timid youth,
coming & going like the migratory birds. Then address the
swallows flitting in their dream like circles speak of the rarity
of the circumstances, that bring together such concords of
men, each man more than himself through whom an unknown life speaks. a circle ever returning into itself . . ."
(Stallworthy 180/81)

The transformation of these already moving lines into the
poem is a master class in how to show, not tell. The manuscripts reveal the "stitching and unstitching" of seemingly
contradictory imagery—bird's flight, compass, dance, a gathering of artists and intellectuals, a house—into a triumphant
unity. Yeats has come a long way from the dreamy youth by
the lake described by Moore, whose talk was more interesting
than his verse. The poetic skin now fits perfectly, the posturing of youth unnecessary. Few scenes in modern poetry are so
well set and few contain such excellent company.

4

THE LONELINESS
OF THE LONG-DISTANCE WRITER

In Dublin recently, I was having a drink when I unexpectedly met a former pupil whom I had taught in the sixties. I told him that I was about to visit my sister's family in West Cork; he invited me to stay with him on my way back through Cork.

"Who would you like to meet in Cork?" he asked.

"Do you realize," I said, "that Cork and environs is infested with my relatives?"

"I see," he said, and we changed the topic and I forgot all about his query. I did, however, remember to turn up on the appointed evening and found myself ushered into a comfortable room full of people I knew but couldn't quite place for a few seconds.

Up piped Aunt Maud: "Timothy, I haven't seen you since 1948. You haven't changed a bit."

My friend's gesture of gathering a dozen or so of my extended family for an exceptionally convivial evening charmed and delighted me, and jolted me into a realization of how much time I had spent away. Lines from "Under Saturn" by Yeats flashed into my head—lines written after a visit to Sligo where Yeats had met an old family retainer:

> 'You have come again,
> And surely after twenty years it was time to come.'
> I am thinking of a child's vow sworn in vain
> Never to leave that valley his fathers called their home.
> (Finneran 179-80)

Sad though this expulsion from a childhood Eden may have been, it remains a constant creative stimulus. To paraphrase Yeats's lines in "The Tower":

> Does the imagination dwell the most
> Upon a [country] won or [country] lost?

The original second line reads: "Upon a woman won or woman lost?" (Finneran 197). The poet is brooding over his unrequited passion for Maud Gonne, balancing that with his fulfillment in marriage. To be part of the Irish diaspora is to have similarly divided loyalties, which nevertheless provide fodder for the imagination in its many ways of being away.

When Lady Gregory was collecting folklore in County Galway in the late nineteenth century, she transcribed stories that told of people being "away"—taken by the fairies. Mrs. Feeney told her: "When one is taken, the body is taken as well as the spirit, and some good-for-nothing thing left in its place." What remains in the "real" world is a "replica." In the days before formal psychiatry, such stories were, no doubt, metaphorical explanations of divided mental states such as schizophrenia. But in a country accustomed to losing many of the most ambitious of its young men and women through emigration—"You might notice it's always the good they take," explained Mrs. Feeney—these stories had profound resonance in relation to "going away." (McDiarmid and Waters 76). No wonder the child in Yeats's early poem "The Stolen Child" is "solemn-eyed": he is leaving the everyday, comforting commonplaces of home:

> Away with us he's going,
> The solemn-eyed:
> He'll hear no more the lowing
> Of the calves on the warm hillside
> Or the kettle on the hob
> Sing peace into his breast
> (Finneran 19)

This little word has resonance in other ways. In many country districts of the British Isles, people still talk of someone being "taken away," a euphemism for madness. John Clare was taken away, having been described by the asylum doctor as "addicted to poetical prosings." In the Maritimes, they say to all outsiders: "You're from away," and this applies as much to a Winnipeger as to a stray Irishman. And my wife tells me that her librarian colleagues talk about vacation time as "awayness" from the office—a term, no doubt, with as much ambiguity as the ubiquitous "out to lunch." Again, in fox hunting, when the fox has broken from covert and is running in the open, the huntsman sounds a motif on the horn called "Gone Away."

In her novel, *Away*, Jane Urquhart relates this Irish folklore to the Canadian experience in a most unusual way. Many artists, including Urquhart, have described the process of being "carried away" by the act of creation, an experience, often euphoric, of mental abstraction in which the customary controlling consciousness is in abeyance. This is sometimes accompanied by what Proust called "involuntary memory" when the mind is unexpectedly flooded with clusters of past sensations time-released into awareness. To be away in this autonomous time is to court misunderstanding and some-times hostility from those who "spend" their time in more conventional ways. This is what the Irish writer Padraic Colum meant by calling the artist a "refugee from time."

The condition of exile is akin to all of the above meanings. The exile is obviously away physically; he or she also leads a double life, which could be interpreted as mentally unstable in that the expatriate has an "away" life and a "replica" life; also, as my aunt's comment implies, an Irish exile is just "out to lunch" and expected back in the office—even if it takes forty years. And this particular expatriate often feels like a fox perpetually chased by the "hounds of time" in full cry—one is out in the open, or overt, with no coverts or hides for protection. The exile confronts in an extreme form the complexity of all choices, when one ponders the "road not taken."

Exile is not just physical, spatial, geographical; it is spiritual, inner, existential. For one can, of course, be alienated from some aspects of one's own country without actually moving away—one can have an alert citizenship every bit as double-barrelled as the expatriate's. Furthermore, one can be alien-ated from many aspects of contemporary culture. Inasmuch as modern society coerces people into various forms of col-lectivity, it becomes incumbent on the writer and poet to refuse the blandishments of superficiality, to live, in Rilke's phrase, "from a deep place." This refusal is political, but it is deeper than any party affiliation or agenda—it is a life's work to sustain the integrity of the self. There is nothing "selfish" about this, for the poetic self includes the universal, impersonal Self as well as the puny individualistic, narcissistic ego. In a world that trades in copies, clones, and replicas, it is a politically engaged act to assert the autonomy of poetry.

There is a passage in the *I Ching* that intrigues me and has indeed become a personal motto: "Work on that which has been spoiled has supreme success." Everyone has spoilings in his or her life, especially perhaps those displaced by exile. The genuine writer's task is to work on those spoilages, those dis-placements, and to re-place them, so that the soul can take root. The experiences of exile, or any kind of awayness, may sometimes spoil the home, but properly channelled, they can bring home the spoils.

5

NICHE WORK IF YOU CAN GET IT

As a professional educator for the past forty-two years, I have read innumerable treatises on the, to me, mysterious process of conveying information/knowledge/wisdom from one psyche to another, also known as teaching. Many of the authors of these articles are convinced that effective teaching is a matter of finding the right set of rules and procedures, and then applying them. The trouble is, however, that the basic rules seem to change every decade or so, leaving students in a parlous state of muddledom. Maybe it is a sign of approaching senility, but I have been pondering my own education recently; what I value about it in retrospect is the almost complete absence of academic theories and of pedagogical procedures. My teachers could at times be lazy, egotistical, arrogant, bad-tempered (my, what rages I have witnessed!), or vain, but they were, for the most part, immersed in their subject matter and hence excellent role models for young people with any intellectual aspirations. If I learned anything during my youth, it seems to have occurred in spite of the above-mentioned human frailties; knowledge was transmitted when nobody was looking, so to speak.

In my first-year English classes, I often get my students to read and discuss Howard Gardner's "A Rounded Version: the Theory of Multiple Intelligences." In this article, Gardner presents his belief, first published in 1983 in the book, *Frames of Mind*, that the traditional IQ tests as devised by Alfred Binet are inaccurate and outmoded. As most of us know from our schooldays, these tests put almost exclusive emphasis on logical/mathematical ability and verbal ability. According to Gardner, these two intelligences, while important, are only part of a broader spectrum of human aptitudes. In 1983, Gardner posited seven branches of intelligence: musical; bodily-kinesthetic; linguistic; logical-mathematical; spatial; interpersonal; and intrapersonal. "Until now," he writes, "we have supported the fiction that adult roles depend largely on the flowering of a single intelligence. In fact, however, nearly every cultural role of any degree of sophistication requires a combination of intelligences" (Jacobus 390). It is the following sentence towards the end of the article that particularly arrests my attention: "An individual may not be particularly gifted in any intelligence; and yet, because of a particular combination or blend of skills, he or she may be able to fill some niche uniquely well" (391).This comment strikes a deep chord in me (and in many of my students). After all, most of us are not king of the castle in any one activity or aptitude, but feel that we can play a courtly or supportive role in the regal economy of complex forces.

To return to my early education: I spent my teenage years (from age thirteen to eighteen) at Saint Columba's College in the foothills of the Dublin mountains about eight miles out of the city. I later went back to teach there for six years, but it is my own schooldays that I want to talk about. I want to provide a self-analysis of someone whom I perceive to be not especially brilliant at any one activity, but who has spent decades trying to orchestrate the intelligences listed above into some kind of harmony. After thirty years or so, I did find a niche professionally, and it paid off all the more richly for the long exploratory period required. I was the despair in my youth of those educational experts, or career counsellors, who asked searching questions along the lines of "What are you going to be when you grow up?" (Their equivalents today talk about "outcomes" and "game-plans" and "windows of opportunity.") I couldn't heave my heart into my mouth to answer along expected lines, such as "I want to join the army" or "I want to become a solicitor" or "I want to make a lot of money": all these were very remote possibilities. At one point, I actually did want to become an engine driver, tormenting my mother with the question: "How does a train engine turn?" (Well, how do you turn around when you've reached the end of the line?) So, really, I hadn't a clue. What I want to do now is examine my school experience in the light of Gardner's theory of multiple intelligences, because the best thing I can say about my schooldays is that I was left alone to work out my own destiny, eccentric as that might have been. I will start with my greatest schoolboy love: music.

In the language of current educational jargon, the "outcome" of my youthful immersion in music had no obvious pay-off—that is, if you are judging as this world wags, and money wags the tail of life. However, how about a life-long and ever-deepening passion for the total output of Johann Sebastian Bach? That has enriched not my pocket, but endlessly enriched my mind. On my desert island, give me my Bach. Your Beethoven and your Mozart are, of course, strong contenders, but if one had to listen to music for six hours a day, every day, Bach's music would never self-destruct. A day without Bach is a day without sunlight.

My first exposure to Bach was listening to Joseph Groocock playing voluntaries as we walked in and out of chapel, twice a day in those days. On feast-days, Sundays, and Saint Columba's Day, Groocock would select a sparkling piece of organ fireworks, such as The Saint Anne Prelude and Fugue. I can still feel the pregnant silence between the ending of the final prayer and blessing and the start of the voluntary. What has he selected? Have I heard it before? How difficult is it? The frustrating part was that one had to walk out of chapel before the piece had unfolded itself, but as we lined up in cloisters for the masters to file past, the music would float tantalisingly over the quadrangle and into my brain for ever. Groocock was our Precentor—choir-master and organist. He used to invite other excellent performers to play in the chapel. I was one of about eight boys privileged to hear the distinguished organist, Lady Susi Jeans. I vividly remember the shoes she was wearing, which found their way around the pedal-board as sure-footed as any thoroughbred. I wrote about it later:

> How can I forget those sensible shoes
> Poised like clogs to trample open that wedge?
> (She was playing Bach's "Wedge" Prelude and Fugue).
> Old-fashioned notes crammed the overloaded score,
> Harnessed like taciturn bunches of fruit,
> Feet, hands expressing a heady vintage,
> Bacchus lurking within Apollo's grove.

*****

She flicks off the reedy flutes and oboes—
Back to *terra firma*—half expecting
Bare feet stained with the mind's purple harvest.

For four years, I sang in the choir, beginning as a treble and leading the choir, taking great joy in anthems such as The Bell Anthem by Purcell and The Mount of Olives by Beethoven. I won a music prize when I was fourteen, playing two piano pieces by Bach from memory, and hoped at that stage that my voice and keyboard performance would mature into something approximating my passion. With puberty, however, came not only self-consciousness but also a crack in the voice and a fissure in the walled garden of my Eden; as my voice moved from treble to alto to tenor to bass, it lost its clarity and bell-like tone. This was my personal fall of man and a primal disappointment. I continued to sing in the choir, however, thus acquiring a knowledge of each part of the harmony, and one of my pleasures remains reading vocal and orchestral scores.

Groocock also taught me to play the piano and organ. Here again, desire outlived performance, but I learned enough about the inner workings of Bach's fugues to fuel my passion for listening to superb performances of Bach and of all music. I also learned discipline from accompanying the choir and congregation (two hundred boys) in hymns and psalms, fascinated by the timing required. When I was fourteen and at a crucial stage of development and impressionability, my father died. That Easter, the choir sang The Saint Matthew Passion by Heinrich Schütz, a predecessor of Bach. The Gospel narrative was recited very beautifully by G. K. White. A few months afterwards, in May 1956, I heard two of the greatest performers of the twentieth century: Louis Armstrong and Yehudi Menuhin. I don't think

51

I've quite recovered yet. Into my grief-saturated ear came tones from another world. "Energy is eternal delight," wrote Blake, and those sound waves are still lapping the shores of my mind. Even Groocock, who was a very intelligent man as well as one of the five or six performers who have made me gasp, could not understand my equal love of those different sounds, as I became head of the Jazz Society and of the Classical Society. I also learned the rudiments of the violin, and sometimes joined an impromptu string quartet with Groocock playing the viola.

In retrospect, music taught me a very valuable skill: the ability to give one's undivided attention to something, also known as concentration. Nowadays, concentration is another of those derided "old-fashioned" skills, revealing one's complete lack of hipness. Even the best modern movies, for example, seem reluctant to allow one to linger for more than a split second on anything—we are carried along on a whirligig of sensation with no time for reflection. In contrast, whenever I listen to the Beethoven Violin Concerto (the first movement is more than twenty-seven minutes long) I am transported back to the music room at school, with its glimpse of Dublin Bay and Howth (where I grew up), the irrigation system for the nearby swimming pool providing its own water music under the window, while down the buttercupped slope, some cricketers might be stealing a few last minutes of twilight as they smacked/dunked/snicked the ball around the pitch where swallows performed arabesques in the rain-scented air. All of these sensuous experiences are, for me, enshrined in the music, a ghostly Braille which has a truly Proustian power to recreate the past.

Another blessing music gave me was the ability to switch from one side of the brain to the other. Music exercises right-brain skills such as intuition and a feeling for wholes rather than fragments. It also exercises several levels of the neural system simultaneously; in music of any complexity, one gets, in Glenn Gould's words, "a simultaneous explosion of ideas." Listening to music, but especially performing it, requires immediate attention to the business at hand (or at foot), the notes themselves; it also requires a subliminal awareness of the whole piece, and the relationship between these micro- and macro-elements. I remember Groocock made me learn the final bars of a fugue before embarking on the opening; in this way, I knew what complexities I was getting into, adjusting the tempo and stop choices accordingly. This left/right brain shuttle is not irrational so much as super-rational; it is a hallmark, I believe, of all great achievement. When Brian Lara beat Sir Garfield Sobers's record of 365 not out for a batsman in a Test Match, he played each ball on its merits—many of them meriting a sound smack to the boundary, but there was an overarching movement in his play as if he were inspired. No wonder, when the great moment came, Lara knelt down and kissed the wicket—"some God was in this place."

Cricket moves us into the second intelligence: bodily-kinesthetic. Up to the age of eighteen, cricket and music took all my love. While sport obviously exercises the body, it does a lot more. In team games especially, one develops eyes in the back of one's head, sensing peripheral strategic movements and making lightning adjustments. Sport is akin to art in that the rules and conditions (weather, pitch, fitness of players) set up certain expectations, which are then frustrated or satisfied by the cut and thrust of the action. I have had moments of pure joy more often in sport than in any other activity. When experience and intuition match favourable conditions, plus a little luck, miracles happen. I once fell slowly sideways to my full length, my outstretched hand receiving a fast-moving ball after its forty-yard parabola. As one gets up on one's feet again after such a perfect moment, one can truly say with Wordsworth in the *Two-Part Prelude*: "The sky seemed not a sky/ Of earth, and with what motion moved the clouds!" (Wu 450)

As with music, I was but an indifferent child of the earth, but I certainly learned enough to relish every moment of great performances, whether in cricket, tennis, rugby, grass hockey, or golf, my schoolboy sports. Sport throws moments of glory at one, followed by moments of humiliation, or vice-versa. One of the defining attributes of major players is their ability to recover from setbacks or momentary incompetence. As Churchill put it: "Success is moving from failure to failure with no loss of enthusiasm." Few early experiences were as devastating, or as existentially didactic, as walking the long trudge back to the pavilion after a low score (or the dreaded "0"—"duck"), with hearty (heartless) comments of "Bad luck, old chap" on all sides. Perhaps the battle of Waterloo was won on the playing fields of Eton. And remember, Samuel Beckett was a very fine cricketer—is *that* where he learned those spine-tingling throwaway remarks? A duck takes the shine off one's bliss, for sure.

Leisure time was more abundant then, so I could indulge these adolescent passions. But I kept my schoolwork in good repair. Meanwhile, the linguistic side of things, to which I have devoted much of my adult life, was lying relatively dormant, but being constantly showered with influences. Just as I absorbed Bach almost unconsciously, so I heard with a detached alertness the doses of the spoken word washing like regular tides over my consciousness. Some time in my late teens, unfocused hearing turned into a grateful listening as words emerged from the fogs of adolescence; with increasing excitement, I intuited the implicit shapes of linguistic artefacts. Whether it was a finely articulated reading of The Prodigal Son in chapel, or singing the Psalms with their simple but sumptuous language, or David Caird reading French and German poetry to us, or David Neligan reading Joyce, or G. K. White reading Cicero, or Maurice Brooks reading Gaelic poetry, or Oisin Kelly reading from *Murder in the Cathedral*, the spoken word acquired a currency in my brain, and added itself to the heady, if confused, rag-bag of sensation I have described above. It was in my final year at school that literature suddenly acquired an urgent presence. The first few lines of "Tintern Abbey" with their subtle repetitions of simple words ("five"; "again") struck me with the force of Holy Writ; *Bleak House* opened an underworld of humane insight. But it was the reflective stateliness of *Persuasion* that had me looking up from the page thinking: How can I spend my life in the company of this marvellous clarity, this "other harmony" of prose? This exposure prepared my mental firmament for further exploration, and it was during my first year at Trinity that the planet Yeats swam into my ken; to change the metaphor, reading Yeats sounded a great gong in my head, which has never stopped reverberating.

If we apply the word "outcome" to this feast of language from which I picked up scraps, it would be impossible to measure the impact it had on a burgeoning consciousness. Thank God, or whatever means the good, that my youthful ear was rinsed clear with this living current. After about a decade, theoretical buzzwords infiltrated the study of literature like a virus, making such remnants of a two-thousand-year oral tradition irrelevant child's-play. The living stream was dammed, and its adherents regarded as heretics. As I approach retirement, I feel enfranchised again, free to do the things I did so naturally in my youth: learn and recite wads of poetry and prose; relish words with an Elizabethan appetite, tasting them on the tongue; maintain a reverence for works of art as autonomous living entities; respect quality in art and life as the *sine qua non* of not only civilized life, but also of any humanly lived existence; make multiple connections between different art-forms; revere excellence in aptitude and performance as a Keatsian "democracy of forest trees." For most of my career, I felt like an outlaw, an adherent of a seemingly discredited system. In the moated fortress of academe, I was ready to hop into a trap door or "priest's hole" when the intellectual inquisitors raided the premises.

My verbal range was further extended by taking part in many drama productions. In the fifties, these were usually not intellectually demanding, but of the happiest-days-of-your-life kind of knockabout. However, like sport, acting created its own discipline of "moving about in worlds unrealized" as I got a taste for the stage and learned to project my otherwise soft voice. Most interesting to me, perhaps, was the way a performer can create a symbiotic relationship with an audience: with a tough audience, the actor has to keep the illusion going against the odds; with a receptive audience, actors can hold the listeners in the palm of their voice. What an excellent training for teaching, as teachers are on stage every working day of their lives, exposed to every kind of audience from the hostile to the adoring (sometimes). And when I took up my first teaching job at the same school, I leaped at the opportunity to direct productions. It was the sixties, and these were often more ambitious (*Doctor Faustus, The Royal Hunt of the Sun*, Yeats, Synge, O'Casey)—in my case, the influence of John Barton at The Royal Shakespeare Company in Stratford was overwhelming.

The master in charge of drama (or I should say, expected to teach drama without remuneration after teaching full-time English) in the fifties and sixties was a diffident character of self-effacing brilliance, David FitzGerald, known fondly as Fitz. His quiet acumen and penetrating irony was another pervasive blessing of my youth. His heroic efforts to keep us marginally cultivated in an atmosphere of largely indifferent philistinism will always be remembered. People forget information, forget even solid learning, but they never forget how someone made them feel—Fitz. made us feel human, endowed us with the lightness of being in the light of enduring things.

Now comes the embarrassing part—the Achilles heel, the unfulfilled, the shadow, the inferior function: logic and mathematics. Not the devil himself and his forefathers could endow me with logic. Mind you, this was partly a creation of my teachers, some of whom, when they scented weakness, went for blood. I remember that I was entranced with the clarity and curvilinear beauty of geometry. On one occasion, I was determined to work out a geometrical problem the master had called particularly tricky. I did it, but when I presented the proof in class, disbelief abounded, and I was not encouraged to continue. Such are the little murders of the schoolroom—my belief in the mathematical, as opposed to the musical, order of the spheres died that day and never returned. As for logic, my mind seems to work in roundabout ways—"by indirections find directions out"—and those used to a straight answer probably find me shiftless and incompetent. So be it. Rather than being perfectly spherical, I seem to be like those balls used in bowling, which are deliberately slanted, out of kilter, and wobbly.

Looking at things from an oblique angle sometimes reveals truths inaccessible to one's straight-down-the-line brethren, like those trick perspectives painted by Holbein and others. I don't want to come across as a liberal arts snob, either, but one whiff of the Chemistry Lab., with its acrid smells, had me running out the door. I suppose that it was evident at an early age that I was less interested in how things worked than in the mysteries of the human psyche. I was an intuitive who valued tuition, but who gave it a spin peculiar to my temperament. Besides, how could I spare one more minute from that sense of continental drift I got when I read great literature?

This brings us to spatial intelligence. In the fantasy game of "Who would you like to have been in history?" if I can't spend a lifetime sending cricket balls scudding along well-mown grass to the boundary like Sobers, or fill Covent Garden with my voice like Placido Domingo, I'd like to be lugging my easel out into another poppy-littered field like Monet and Renoir. Or I'd turn up at an estate, like Capability Brown, and say: "This terrain has capabilities, my Lord." The spaced-out nature of things has always fascinated me, whether it be a thousand-acre estate or a Japanese garden or a window box. Similarly, the way artists portray space intrigues me: a philosopher on a misty Chinese mountain or a sun-drenched Renoir meadow or a Braque abstract or a Corot painting of Chartres Cathedral. The individual's mysterious relationship with space and place is one of my abiding fascinations. My attraction to the poetry of John Clare, for example, goes beyond the linguistic or literary in that Clare sees with an infinity of eyes. Clare, like the great painters, teaches us that we do not stand in front of experience as if we are looking at a framed picture, but move through it, growing eyes like an old potato.

While my discovery of Clare came long after my schooldays, the gaping needs of my visual/spatial/environmental senses were endlessly nourished in the fortuitous setting of the college. Saint Columba's was surrounded by beautiful scenery, the foothills of the Dublin and Wicklow mountains. On half holidays, one had the choice of watching the rugby match (in winter), or the cricket match (in summer), or taking off for a ramble, up the bumpy track called the Hurley Lane, which after five hundred yards or so brought one out to the slopes of wild mountain country, with half-ruined cottages, sheep, roaring torrents, and great splashes of gorse. This was quintessential John Millington Synge country. Below, the sweeping curve of Dublin Bay stretched from Dalkey to "Howth Castle and environs," the city itself nestled around the Liffey estuary. Occasionally, one had to take part in a competitive cross-country run for eight miles or more, which gave one's exhausted vision a speeded-up version of these superb landscapes. Even a light fall of snow would send crowds of boys up the hillside with makeshift toboggans, like a scene out of Brueghel. And on one occasion, I accompanied a daredevil older boy on an apple-raiding expedition into Marlay Grange, the local big estate. We clambered over stone walls, reconnoitred our way through long grass and brambles, eventually plucking the ripe apples with a scarcely-conscious guilty pleasure. Such trespass of space and place was all part of my personal Garden of Eden.

Art class was presided over by the patriarchal, spade-bearded figure of Oisin Kelly, at the time Ireland's foremost living sculptor. He was of the old school, all right, with no glad sufferance of fools, making it clear anyway that he regarded most of us as "pampered jades." But one stroke of his pencil could put one's halting scribbles on their way to coherence. He probably wouldn't get a job in this politically correct age, but his mere presence and devotion to the art/craft was worth its weight in oil paint. Like Groocock, he was a learned man in other respects, and snatches of great poetry would fall nonchalantly from his lips just as the wood shavings curled and fell. I always remember his acerbic pronunciation of the word "partly" in Eliot's line: "Living and partly living." There was no part-time living in Oisin Kelly's presence.

Another aspect of the spatial intelligence I must mention is my love of maps. I could "read" maps for hours at a time, getting lost in contours and colours and the interconnecting network of villages, roads, rivers, railways, canals, what have you. This is another largely extra-curricular activity, but I must acknowledge my geography teachers, including Norman Lush, who first acquainted me with this language of outer spaces. My love of Ireland was greatly enhanced by those old maps with their "coloured counties." The older the map, the better it nourishes the imagination. I have an original Speed map at home, dated 1610, which even has a sea monster emerging from the billows in the vicinity of Wexford.

Two other amateur interests have their origin in this "fair seed-time"—landscape gardening and architecture. The older school buildings were a mixture of Georgian and Victorian Gothic (I will not expatiate on the quality of some of the more modern buildings, but I remember the adjective "excremental" being applied). To live and work in older settings is to imbibe knowledge in a way that I call "learning by osmosis," which is another way of saying that even when one is not consciously "looking," one is taking things in subliminally. This makes history more easily come alive in one's imagination, let alone giving a small insight into the architect's mind. One of my cousins is a retired architect, and I have walked with him around such places as Trinity College, Dublin and Oxford. He would point out curves, gable ends, ornamentation and the management of visual surprises that sharpened my observations and enriched my understanding. As for landscape gardening, the relationship of the gardens to the buildings always intrigued me at school, and fed a later passion for perambulating landscape gardens in France, England, and Ireland. And I am fortunate enough to have a mini-landscape garden of my own, where the levels, gradients, textures, colours, plantings, and seasonal changes keep my mind refreshed from its usual overdose of the printed word.

This brings us to interpersonal intelligence, also known as people skills. Arguably, this is the most important of all. People get hired and fired ostensibly for their professional competence or otherwise. But the real reason is nearly always that they have turned someone on or rubbed someone the wrong way. A colleague of mine has admitted that it was the timely and appropriate joke I told in the interview that clinched my present appointment—it was one of those happy coincidences of the right comment at the right time to the right people. And we all know the opposite feeling—that in spite of endless preparation, the spirit of the moment is wrong. While I have always tried to keep the peace with most people, it is a strain because I am by nature an introvert and constantly misunderstood or misread. I am, on the whole, a born teacher, but my natural tendency to introversion means that the constant stage presence required of a teacher is a huge expenditure of energy. I also need long periods of solitude and meditation to keep my perspective. However, provided I can keep reserves of confidence, talking to and interacting with people energises me, and boarding school developed this aptitude. My Irishness also contributes to this intelligence—there have been times when I have literally talked all night rather than get some sleep.

Introverts, Jung's word for those people with what Howard classifies as intrapersonal skills, usually have a hard time of it at boarding schools. However, as I have mentioned, my poetic side was on hold, and I escaped the malign attentions of bullies and other unsavoury denizens of such places by playing sport every day. I was a "good citizen," opening doors for masters and retreating with a slight bow as Matron swept past with her nun-like coif. But boarding school is dedicated to cutting one down to size; remarks such as "You're not the only pebble on the beach" were common. When I read about the torments Shelley was subjected to at Eton, I am glad that my arty side never became "precious"—good training for later life, as society has scant respect for the kind of exhaustive introspection required of the poet. But Saint Columba's was softer and kinder than what I've heard about English boarding schools—in spite of a stringent discipline, it didn't take itself too seriously. Not only did Ireland have no Empire to run, but also Protestant Irish people grew up in a strange political vacuum. In Southern Ireland, we constituted a tiny and diminishing minority (4%). So, external conditions conspired to teach me a healthy discipline, but allowed me time to dream.

People with strong intrapersonal skills are often assumed to be mere dreamers. But this intelligence is perhaps the most demanding of all. It requires self-discipline and self-aware-ness. It takes on the huge task described by Jung's theory of individuation—a lifetime of becoming the person you potentially are, the alchemical process of converting the raw materials of one's teeming molecules into something compe-tent, if not significant. Saint Columba's gave me the psychic space to get this process rolling; I learned the value of inde-pendence along with interdependence and my teachers en-couraged the working out of my own salvation. I mentioned earlier that self-consciousness was the demon that destroyed my illusions of being a musical whizkid; the struggle with this demon is essential for a mature being. Yet, to do any-thing well requires a self-forgetting, a happy oblivion from care and absence of deliberation. Managing this paradox has been for me a life-long fascination, and my schooldays pro-vided me with a model of such a paradox.

Intrapersonal intelligence has the added difficulty of forcing one to confront one's dark side, what Jung calls the Shadow. The shadow side of things is essential to a balanced life, as night is to day. One of the most memorable German texts I studied with David Caird was *Peter Schlemihl*, in which the protagonist sells his shadow to the devil (who kneels down and rolls it up like a carpet). Losing one's shadow is akin to losing one's soul. But like all soul work, the shadow in oneself is a challenge, and often downright disreputable. I recently attended a lecture on Jung where the lecturer ad-mitted that her shadow side revealed itself when she got irri-tated by someone jumping ahead in a line-up. I'm afraid my shadow side is a lot scarier than that—I often scare myself with my own desert places, like Frost. Perhaps artists are es-pecially prone to these swings: beautiful as Dante's *Paradiso* is, his *Inferno* has the authentic touch indeed.

Boarding schools can be infernal places (in the sixties it became fashionable to describe them as mini-concentration camps), but I was lucky. On the whole, Saint Columba's was a humane place. I am not a parent, but from talking to parents about the triumphs and disasters of their children's experiences, schooling seems to be a chancy business. Eton and Oxford are no guarantee against human nature; conversely, great achievement can arise in the most unpromising conditions. For better or for worse, the seeds so liberally and informally scattered during those crucial years under the shadow of Kilmashogue (the local mountain) and within sight of the Hell-Fire Club (the ruins of an eighteenth-century place of debauchery) have made up the being that I am.

The foregoing reminiscences are very impressionistic. I have attempted to extract some principles from them, as follows:

1. Knowledge cannot be neatly divided into compartments or rooms: it is all one house.
2. The education of the senses is as important as the education of the intellect.
3. Focused development of one branch of intelligence enhances the other branches.
4. The greatest blessing one can take away from authentic education is the power of paying attention.
5. Education, to be of life-long benefit, must expose the students to greatness in every field.
6. The ambitious student will always seek out brilliant practitioners. While this can be intimidating, it is sensible to study models of excellence, as they set the bar for all subsequent evaluation.

7. Constant exercise of the body is as important as exercise of the mind and senses.

8. Education should not produce "know-alls." The most highly trained people in every field are always working at an unknown frontier. While my education was within the Anglican Communion, even a secular education should take upon it the mystery of things.

9. Authentic education is humane, not mechanical. If its most obvious aim is to enable people to earn a living, its real purpose is to make that life worth living. As Robert Graves once observed: There may not be much money in poetry, but there isn't much poetry in money, either.

10. Teachers, like other professionals, can only point the way. The most important lesson they can convey is: "It's up to YOU."

6

RANDOM REFLECTIONS
ON LITERATURE AND TEACHING

To define is necessary, but it is also to limit. Good teachers, like good artists, need to find a vocabulary for the indefinable.

Teachers are, to some extent, involved in tuition: that is, the imparting of a body of knowledge. They should be even more involved in intuition: a feeling for mystery, beauty, and contradiction.

Classroom time: the tip of the iceberg. I once tried to work out the ratio of invisible to visible person-hours in teaching—it came out at forty to one. However, no government official seems qualified to understand this.

Students need passion and compassion. You can learn all the techniques you like, but without those two ingredients in your teaching you are as "a sounding brass or a tinkling cymbal."

Every class is a performance. Yes, and requires the same commitment to practice as singing opera does.

5.

The teacher, of course, should never become a prima donna. A more appropriate analogy is that of the conductor of an orchestra or choir—he or she sets the pace, rhythms, and dynamics, but it is the students who are the players and singers.

Students need sincerity: they like to feel that the teacher is honest. They also need authenticity: they like to know that the teacher has made leaps in the dark such as they may want to make.

All students are (of course) equal, but some are more equal than others because they take responsibility for their learning.

Seasoned teachers say that the first class is the most important of the whole semester. I would go further and say that students make a decision about the quality of the class within fifteen to thirty seconds of the teacher's first words.

Teachers should constantly monitor the ratio between sparkling pupils and glazed eyes—if the deadpans outnumber the sparks, they should change their techniques or plan early retirement.

Yeats once wrote in a letter late in his life: "Man can embody truth but he cannot know it . . . You can refute Hegel but not the Saint or the Song of Sixpence." (Jeffares 290-91). Many teachers, who have invested heavily in rational cognition, should ponder such statements.

Each class should not just cover "content"; it should provide a hologram of the whole course.

All true scholars are self-taught, but good teachers have given them a self to believe in.

All good teachers are self-taught, and students have given them a self to believe in.

"There is a Moment in each Day that Satan cannot find . . ." (from Blake's *Milton*). Teachers are the guardians of those moments.

The main aim of education: to train the attention. Attention relieves the modern malady of "the strained time-ridden faces/ Distracted from distraction by distraction." (from Eliot's *Four Quartets*.)

The Tao of teaching: less is better than more.

The Swiss Cheese Method of teaching: take your content and knock holes in it so the students can inspire (breathe in) and be inspired (feel co-creators of the material).

The aim of each class: to create a community. I use this word in what might be called an ecological sense—an awareness of the interconnectedness of each part to the whole.

The word ecology comes from the Greek word "oikos", meaning home. To teach in a connected way is to make students at home in the subject and at home in the world.

There has been a lot of fuss made about the separation of The Two Cultures (sciences and arts). Good teaching should aim to heal the more radical separation of the two meanings of the word "Culture"—the cultivation of the earth and the cultivation of our minds. The most abstruse thought should have a whiff of green fields about it.

We teach what we are. If you wear a teacher's hat during work hours and a citizen's hat at home, students will pick up the false vibes.

Most teachers are burnt out by the age of sixty. The shame of it is that they may have just become eligible to teach by that age.

All teachers should lament the modern suppression of a great art: the art of reading (or reciting) out loud. This is another passive-aggressive tool of literate cultures to marginalize oral cultures or of adults to keep children quiet.

"All art aspires towards the condition of music." (Walter Pater). This applies no less to the art of teaching. My personal ritual: two hours of J. S. Bach per day. My passion for Beethoven, dating from hearing the opening bars of Piano Concerto No. 3 when I was twelve, makes me over-excited; Bach arranges mysterious mandalas of sand on the stretched drum of my nerves.

What place does literature have in education? It has a central place, because it develops and nourishes the Imagination.

What is Imagination? The Imagination blends the intellect with the feelings, it enables opposites to co-exist, creates a state of mind akin to deep meditation: a stillness without stagnation, a detachment without apathy, a clarity without glibness, and an inner violence without harmfulness.

Within the Western tradition, Shakespeare is unrivalled for scope and depth of Imagination. Here is Shakespeare on Imagination:

> And as imagination bodies forth
> The forms of things unknown, the poet's pen
> Turns them to shapes, and gives to airy nothing
> A local habitation and a name.
> (Wells and Taylor, *Early Comedies*, 395)

Imagination includes the wisdom of the body, probes the unknown, is a shaping power, roots experience in the local, and enables us to dwell in the habitual clothed with significance.

The Imagination in action? Try Cleopatra on Antony:

> For his bounty,
> There was no winter in't; an autumn 'twas,
> That grew the more by reaping. His delights
> Were dolphin-like; they showed his back above
> The element they lived in. In his livery
> Walked crowns and crownets. Realms and islands were
> As plates dropped from his pocket.
> (Wells and Taylor, *Classical Plays*, 367-8)

In one of the most memorable passages of *The Prelude*, Wordsworth writes:

> I said unto the life which I had lived,
> 'Where art thou? Hear I not a voice from thee
> Which 'tis reproach to hear?' Anon I rose
> As if on wings, and saw beneath me stretched

Vast prospect of the world which I had been,
And was . . .
(Jonathan Wordsworth et al. 478)

This, in my experience, is how works of imagination affect us: there is a brief expansion and elevation of being, a magnification of the soul (as in "My soul doth magnify the Lord"), but there is also a humbling self-judgement involving mental discipline.

To deny anyone access to such stuff is a deprivation of the most basic kind.

Anthologies are necessary, but they have a deadening effect—the same old chestnuts keep turning up. Every teacher of literature should have a personal anthology, which might be as eccentric as teachers often are.

Many courses nowadays compel the teacher to condense a vast amount of content into, say, twelve three-hour classes. It can be done, but takes very patient and long-term preparation. I have heard the famous scholar M. H. Abrams speak for a whole hour on eight lines of Wordsworth. Better that miniaturized clarity than the "lunch in Paris" syndrome; however, the Grand Tour approach can also be very rewarding, and who ever said that lunch in Paris was a waste of time?

Literature releases us from "single vision and Newton's sleep" (Blake's description of materialism), and enables us to participate in what Dr. Johnson called "the broad sunshine of life."

What are called "minor" works are often more perfect in their way than the accepted masterpieces. A lyric by, say, A. E. Housman, cannot hold a candle to the refulgent agonies of *King Lear*, but both experiences are necessary for a well-rounded reader.

Students should be encouraged not only to read at different speeds but also at different weights, so to speak. To use boxing terminology, some books are heavyweights, some lightweights, some bantamweights, and so on. But as with "minor" works, "light" reading can be both entertaining and enlightening.

The contemporary prejudice against learning by heart is misguided and wasteful. Knowledge relies on memory chastened by experience; if nothing is memorized, what remains is an undigested welter of impressions.

Self-expression: to the novice student this word denotes a release of personal emotion. Education in the arts is an attempt to convert personal emotion into impersonal feeling. Personal emotions are necessary, but they are only the raw materials of art.

T. S. Eliot once wrote that poets are committed by their profession to turn the unpoetical into poetry. Teachers are committed by their profession to convert intractable materials into teachable ones. All texts are teachable, but it takes a lot of knowledge and skill to set up the right contexts.

Students should be given plenty of time to fall in love with their favourite writers. Too many books and articles in the past thirty years have been written by people who seem never to have loved literature. Critics, with some honourable exceptions, have become an arrogant tribe whose aggressiveness has too often ignored or obscured the power and beauty of original works. As intellectual micro-climates change, nothing is more dated than the political imperatives of one or two decades ago.

If students have to read the work of critics, the teacher should guide them to the bracing clarity of good scholars and steer them away from the posturings of those feathering their nests in the name of some fashionable ideology. All revolutions commit excesses and students may have to be reminded that we don't *have* to read the unreadable.

Being human, we are always swayed in our choice of reading by our likes and dislikes. The mature reader, however, balances those egotisms against the need for a broad perspective. In discussing the French Revolution debate, for example, many teachers ignore the work of Edmund Burke, who functions for them at best as a kind of bogey-man. That Burke is one of the great intellects of English Literature, with a style to match, seems to them irrelevant. It was that other great intellect, Samuel Johnson, who maintained that, when he was feeling low, meeting Burke would kill him—"That fellow calls forth all my powers"—so perpetual was Burke's "stream of mind." (Fleeman 696)

Cultivated readers always have this question—one asked by Simon Schama in relation to landscape—at the back of their minds: "When we look at a work of literary art, do we see Nature or Culture?" This applies especially to Shakespeare, who is like the voice of Nature itself.

Writers may not always be the best teachers, but they are first-hand witnesses of the soul-making mental earthquakes that shift them from craft to technique. Technique is that quality in writing that makes it undergo a sea-change into something rich and strange, from words bunched up on a page to words through which a mysterious force moves, greater than the writer consciously intends.

The teacher of literature should convey a passion for the subject, a broad tolerance of different styles and viewpoints, an awareness of the writers' techniques, and above all, a respect for all good pieces of writing as autonomous works of art impervious to the prejudices we may bring to them. True works have many incarnations according to the obsessions of each period, but they remain "monuments more lasting than brass."

What have I learned from a lifetime of teaching? (I began my first teaching job in 1963). That teaching is the most difficult and most undervalued art—if you think you've begun to master it, you're lost. It reminds me of what a wag said about Irish history—if you think you've got the facts, you've certainly been misinformed.

I have also learned that my first instincts were on track: I wanted to teach because I sensed an undercurrent in myself that wanted releasing; because poetry had seized me by the scruff of the neck and I felt impelled to go and do likewise in the name of poetry; because literature seemed the only way to throw bridges across the endless visible and invisible divisions of Irish life in particular and of life in general; because the best students always inhabit the Land of the

Young, whether they are sixteen or sixty; and because everything else seemed a waste of life by comparison.

Works of literature are made with words—writers are first of all craftspeople working in the forge of language, artisans. Good writers are also technicians of the soul, venturing into the worlds beyond words, into the "dim inane" as Shelley called it. Sometimes they are driven mad by the quest, sometimes they sail back with their holds crammed with bullion—riches not wrested from a poorer possessor but stored in the mind like golden grain to contribute to the harvest of the broader culture.

I have learned that the two fields I have cultivated—Irish Literature and Romantic Literature—are galleons lumbering with riches. I may live in an actual country, but I can only dwell in the landscapes of those ancient townlands, those parochial jurisdictions whose labourers broadcast their word-seed in timeless rhythms and universal gestures.

A true work of art is inexhaustible. In the mid-nineteenth century, Matthew Arnold formulated his theory of "touchstones"—those works to which we return again and again, finding them forever fresh. I prefer the concept outlined in Keats's letter to John Taylor of 30 January 1818: "I assure you that when I wrote it, it was a regular stepping of the Imagination towards a Truth. My having written that Argument will perhaps be of the greatest Service to me of any thing I ever did—It set before me at once the gradations of Happiness even like a kind of Pleasure Thermometer." (Gittings, *Letters*, 59)

Who registers on my thermometer? Too numerous to mention, but among the chief are: Shakespeare, Wordsworth,

Yeats, Synge, Heaney, Keats, Blake, Chaucer, Ronsard, Baudelaire, Rilke, Whitman, Dante, Clare, Woolf, Hardy, Dickinson . . . These are the inexhaustibles, among a host of others. These pioneers of the Imagination are also corner-stones of what used to be called a liberal education. Whatever one calls it, a detailed immersion in any of these contributes to that ecosystem we call a free mind, "whose service is perfect freedom."

7

BALANCING ACTS

Those working in the creative arts seem to be instinctively aware of what mathematicians and architects call the Golden Section, also known as the Golden Ratio, the Golden Mean, and the Divine Proportion. These terms refer to a principle, found everywhere in nature from mollusks to the human face, that objects are not packaged symmetrically but arrest our attention by slightly skewed ratios of mass, balance, and surprise. The Divine Proportion is described by Bülent Atalay in his book *Math and the Mona Lisa* as when "the whole is to the major part as the major part is to the minor," and it is expressed mathematically by phi=1.618.

Recording technicians once plotted the graph of a piece of music by Hildegard of Bingen, and found it to be in the shape of the Golden Section. The ineffable beauty of Bach's cantata arias is also made up of similar sound-shapes; if an aria is five minutes long, something mysterious and unpredictable often occurs about three and a half minutes into the piece. Have you ever seen a tree that was perfectly symmetrical? It seems that nature can never be boring, and this slight deviation from equipoise is one of its secrets. It is therefore no surprise that artists, whether consciously or not, have emulated this craftiness in nature.

In literature, the Italian sonnet has a built-in imbalance: an octave of eight lines is followed by a sestet of six lines (how boring it would be if it were 7/7). While the English sonnet, with its three quatrains and a couplet is perhaps more straightforward, it also can play see-saw with the laws of equilibrium. And some of the finest sonnets in English are a blend of the two archetypes. One of the most perfect sonnets I know is "The Silken Tent" by Robert Frost, first published in *A Witness Tree* (1942):

> She is as in a field a silken tent
> At midday when a sunny summer breeze
> Has dried the dew and all its ropes relent,
> So that in guys it gently sways at ease,
> And its supporting central cedar pole,
> That is its pinnacle to heavenward
> And signifies the sureness of the soul,
> Seems to owe naught to any single cord,
> But strictly held by none, is loosely bound
> By countless silken ties of love and thought
> To everything on earth the compass round,
> And only by one's going slightly taut
> In the capriciousness of summer air
> Is of the slightest bondage made aware.

Frost reproduces in his craft the subject-matter of this poem: there is a breath-taking balance between fluidity and tautness, the guy-ropes slackening and tightening to keep the whole entity floating in its own buoyancy. And what a touching love poem, its awareness of bonds, boundaries, and limits a launching pad for affection. Perhaps only an

American poet could get away with the charming pun, "So that in guys it gently sways at ease." This lady navigates her way with a sure compass; the give and take of relationships is managed with an insouciance that is really a refined balancing act.

This give and take is beautifully echoed in the impulsion of the verse: it is all one sentence, yet there is no sense of being out of breath as one reads or recites this poem. The metre and the rhyme scheme follow the English pattern exactly, yet we are not aware of the slightest bondage to convention. And the "but" at the beginning of line 9 is in keeping with the "turn" or "volta" of the Italian sonnet, but it is such a slight change of direction that the poem continues to sway at ease.

If poems are houses, huts, hermitages, hiding places, then this sonnet is designed by an architecture of affection; it is a blueprint of how things ought to be. The soul is well housed, accommodated, pegged to the earth but spreading its sails to the breeze. The proprietor of this tent, who is potentially everyone, is analogous to Ben Jonson's ideal proprietor in "To Penshurst":

> Now, Penshurst, they that will proportion thee
> With other edifices, when they see
> Those proud, ambitious heaps, and nothing else,
> May say, their lords have built, but thy lord dwells.
> (Abrams et al. Vol. I, 1225)

A similar balancing act of content and technique is evident in another sonnet of love, "The Master Speed," first published in *A Further Range: Book Six* (1936):

No speed of wind or water rushing by
But you have speed far greater. You can climb
Back up a stream of radiance to the sky,
And back through history up the stream of time.
And you were given this swiftness, not for haste
Nor chiefly that you may go where you will,
But in the rush of everything to waste,
That you may have the power of standing still—
Off any still or moving thing you say.
Two such as you with such a master speed
Cannot be parted nor be swept away
From one another once you are agreed
That life is only life forevermore
Together wing to wing and oar to oar.

This sonnet is also a judicious blend of the Italian and English forms. It has three rhyming quatrains and a rhyming couplet, as in Shakespeare, and it uses the octave/sestet break or turn (volta) brilliantly to enhance the theme—for example, there is a moment of stasis at the end of line 8 (end of octave) matching the words "standing still." This equilibrium is thrown out of kilter by the fact that the meaning runs on into line 9, thus upsetting the weighing scales of the poem. After this ralentando, the final five lines sweep us away in one breath and with no punctuation. This enhances the theme because "Two such as you" are speedier than one.

This brings us to the word "speed." Our natural reaction is to associate this word with rush, quickness, motion of all kinds. However, further readings force on us an older meaning of the word—speed meaning good fortune, success, furtherance: the primary meanings listed in the *OED*. This is an ancient use of the word, coming from Old English and Old High German, and surviving, if it survives at all in our materialistic age, in such expressions as "God speed," "Christ be our speed," and the Shakespearean "Good manners be your speed."

Far from being a rush job, this poem stands and delivers. It is not about velocity, but about stability; not about swift currents, but lasting currency; not about streams, but streams of consciousness; not about being fast, but being steadfast; not quick but quickening; not motion but emotion; not the quicksands of actuality but the quickset hedges of hope; not running to seed but running to paradise; not the revolving wheel window of the Primum Mobile, but the energized stillness of the Rose Window of the Empyrean. In short, to use Simone Weil's words, it is not about gravity but about grace.

My students and I have noticed how Seamus Heaney encourages the reader to regard language as a series of geological deposits containing linguistic, mythical, local, and dialectical layers. To analyse a poem, then, is to dig for gold, and it is up to the readers to pan it out in the sieves of their understandings. By digging into the layers of the word "speed," we quicken (bring to life) the core of this poem, which would remain partly obscure without the resonances in that word.

This is a poem about imagination—how it holds up a higher power, a "radiance" against mere consumerism ("the rush of everything to waste"), creating a spiritual flight formation (wing to wing) and seaworthy vessel (oar to oar). The alert reader will pick up the modern meaning of "speed" in line 1, but the ancient meaning in line 2. The literary reader will pick up an echo of Blake's passage in *Milton* describ-

81

ing souls meeting "wing-tip to wing-tip." Proverbial echoes include "Speed is of the Devil" and *"Festina lente"* / "Make haste slowly."

This masterly sonnet of flowing natural energies arrested in a brooding stillness has a great precursor in Wordsworth's final River Duddon sonnet:

> I thought of thee, my partner and my guide,
> As being past away. Vain sympathies!
> For *backward*, Duddon, as I cast my eyes,
> I see what was, and is, and will abide;
> Still glides the stream, and shall forever glide;
> The form remains, the function never dies,
> While we, the brave, the mighty, and the wise,
> We men who, in our morn of youth, defied
> The elements, must vanish; be it so!
> Enough, if something from our hands have power
> To live, and act, and serve the future hour;
> And if, as tow'rd the silent tomb we go,
> Through love, through hope, and faith's transcendent
>   dower,
> We feel that we are greater than we know.
> (Wu 578)

Addresses (apostrophes) to water sources—springs, fountains, rivers—have an ancient pedigree, sometimes called riparian verse (Latin: *ripus*, a river bank). Equally ancient is the metaphor of rivers as the life-giving veins of the earth. For the Romantics, rivers are powerful emblems of the workings of the mind: springs are associated with inspiration, waterfalls (cataracts) with the abyss, meanders with recollection as the mind rounds on itself. Running water is energizing, both physically and mentally. Rivers are also metaphors for life itself, rising in a dark cavern, wandering through varied landscapes, and disappearing into the ocean of eternity. Water is simultaneously an emblem of flux and of stability: "Still glides the stream, and shall for ever glide."

Wordsworth and Coleridge loved to trace rivers to their sources, and associate the "tints" and sounds of rivers with their earliest experience. The great projected philosophical poem Coleridge was always exhorting Wordsworth to write was initially going to be called "The Brook." The river, along with winds/breezes and clouds, is one of the central images in *The Prelude*. Wordsworth describes his soul as "a rock with torrents roaring" (Jonathan Wordsworth et al. 470), in a passage paying tribute to his sister, Dorothy. The passage concludes with a beautiful multiple pun, where the word "spring" can mean a spring in the step, the source of the river of his life and inspiration, and the season that softens the winter of his discontent: "Thy breath,/Dear sister, was a kind of gentler spring/That went before my steps." (Jonathan Wordsworth et al. 472). Most crucially, when he despondently casts around for an anchoring image to convey the depth of his past, it is the "voice" of the River Derwent that sends him triumphantly on his way: "Was it for this/ That one, the fairest of all rivers, loved/ To blend his murmurs with my nurse's song,/ And from his fords and shallows, sent a voice/ That flowed along my dreams?" (Jonathan Wordsworth et al. 42)

The River Duddon in this sequence of sonnets is for Wordsworth what Byzantium is for Yeats, where golden birds sing of "what is past, or passing, or to come." The Duddon, when seen in visionary retrospection, is an earnest of "what was, and is, and will abide." Both metaphors plumb deep resonances in their minds, enabling them to gather in one

83

volume the scattered leaves of their experience, to use a Dantean metaphor. In fact, Byzantium and the River Duddon function as does Beatrice for Dante, as a spiritual guide, and one that requires a transcendence of ordinary cognition:

> *E cosi, figurando il paradiso,*
> *Convien saltar lo sacrato poema,*
> *Come chi trova suo cammin riciso.*
> (*Paradiso*, Canto xxiii)

["And so, picturing Paradise/ The sacred poem must make a leap/ Like one that finds his path cut off."] (Sinclair 333)

Beatrice, the golden birds, and the river all make the poets "feel that we are greater than we know." In Canto xxx of the Paradiso, Dante consolidates this leap, and he uses a river to describe the ultimate vision of bliss:

> *Me sormontar di sopr'a mia virtute . . .*
> *E vidi lume in forma di rivera*
> *Fulvido di fulgore, intra due rive*
> *Dipinte di mirabel primavera.*

["I was conscious of rising beyond my own powers . . . And I saw light in the form of a river pouring its splendour between two banks painted with marvellous spring."] (Sinclair 433)

Wordsworth here, as always, employs echoes of the great Italian poet, and his sonnet is more Italian than English in form. Once again, the off-balance nature of the Italian sonnet is emphasized by being divided semantically into the first nine lines and the concluding five lines. So the members of what Keats called the "immortal freemasonry" of poetry echo each other. They are able to do so by intuitively understanding the laws of geometry and physics, in learning to proportion their poem-dwellings with other edifices.

8

CASTING OFF MUDDY VESTURES

The Florentine author, Machiavelli (1469-1527), tells us that his reverence for the classics was such that "when evening comes I return home and go into my study. On the threshold I strip off my muddy, sweaty workaday clothes and put on the robes of court and palace, and in this graver dress I enter the courts of the ancients and am welcomed by them. And for the space of four hours . . . I pass indeed into their world." (*The Panorama of the Renaissance*, ed. Margaret Aston. London: Thames and Hudson, 1996).

Here the writer of an infamous treatise advising princes to behave expediently rather than ethically has a different message for us all. We often say nowadays things like: "Where has respect gone?" or "Nothing is sacred anymore." But is this true? I believe the modern and post-modern habit of trashing everything in sight is proving to be both boring and counter-productive, especially to the young. Whatever our beliefs, we need something to live for and to live by. However workaday our normal activities, however grubby our usual habits, we need exemplars of such quality that they compel us to divest ourselves of the mundane and redress ourselves to enter "the courts of the ancients."

What do I live by? What, in addition to the obvious activities of keeping body and soul together by getting and spending, do I return to again and again? Apart from my Irish heritage, which is a constant obsession, I return to those works of art that have sustained and fortified me for, in some cases, five decades or more. My professional life was devoted to literature, especially poetry, but poetry was a late-comer in my youthful development. Music came first.

In the spring of 1954, when I was twelve and living at our farm in County Wicklow, my sister brought home from Dublin a recording on 78 rpm records of Beethoven's Piano Concerto Number 3. In those days, it took several records to get through a movement, let alone a whole work, and after a few weeks, there was an accompanying crackle of scratches. No matter. From the opening chords, simple yet mysterious ascending thirds, I was swept into the tides of Beethoven's turbulent mind with its breath-taking moments of calm like sunlight between storm clouds. If ever a sensibility lay waiting for the right sounds to match its incoherent confusions and dreams, this was a match made in purgatory, the purgatory of awakening adolescence. Furthermore, my father was ill with TB, and many a day, I saw the doctor's battered old Ford negotiating the puddles of our long country drive, and knew that my mother had feared for the worst upstairs.

My mind at that time was soft wax that was imprinted with the slightest sensation or experience. Music is constantly playing in my head—actually listening to it or reading scores just focuses a process that goes on all the time. I was fortunate in that what I heard became a lasting blessing and set the tone for all else. Beethoven dominated my teenage years: the building of huge expectation, followed by shattering disillusion, the building of tension and the release of tension, a kind of prolonged and sublimated sexuality. The infinite longing of that music has matured over time into a dignified but melancholy dance to the music of time. Nothing, however, can remove the freshness of those images originally called forth by the music, partly mental constructs, partly vivid impressions of my immediate surroundings. So, as that first movement gains its sea-swell momentum, what do I see?

I see through the big window of the sitting-room the gravel expanse before the front door, the steps leading up to the main sloping lawn (built by Jim three years afterwards for a wedding), the curve of the drive which, thirty yards away, goes under an archway created by an overgrown creeper acting as the entrance to the garden surrounding the house. Just after 3:00 o'clock on week days, when autumn or winter light is already thickening, the postman free-wheels down the drive on his rickety bicycle and goes round the back to the kitchen door, usually greeted by Nan, Mrs. Lambert, or Mrs. Cullen. (It was several years later that the Wicklow County Council provided such men with motorised scooters—their route was miles of hilly roads in all weathers). I see Jim Canavan, who walked up every working day from Avoca village, ushering the four cows in to be milked. Jim kept lawns, gravel, and garden looking spruce, and presided over the greenhouse with its green and purple grapes and the kitchen garden with vegetables and flowers growing side by side.

Occasionally, my father felt well enough to walk in the garden, either to show guests the roses or to make a note of ivy getting too vigorous on certain trees. My mother often accompanied him arm in arm—after thirty years of marriage with many setbacks, they were like young lovers. Mrs. Cullen lived a few hundred yards down the path that went through the Ballyarthur woods to Avoca; I sometimes went down to their cottage in the evening with Nan or her husband, Bartle, to sip strong tea and sit silently looking into the coal fire, letting the local gossip and story-telling, accompanied by several loudly ticking clocks, wash over me. Nan and Bartle lived in a cottage in the farmyard until my father died in 1956; they returned to Baldoyle, not ever fully taking to country ways. The likes of Mrs. Cullen would say: "Yous are only runners-in."

The slow movement starts. Slow-motion playbacks now crowd my head: David Plunkett's father, who always wore slippers even when visiting, bringing his car to a halt by crunching into the wall between the front door and the drawing-room windows . . . Nan coming to the outer half-door of the pantry to greet Edwina, the donkey. Edwina, who was usually munching in a corner of the ten-acre field, would saunter down to the back door at tea-time and pound the door with her hoof . . . Nan pushing my mother down the two steps outside my parents' bedroom after my father slipped away; they had had a twenty-hour vigil: "Ma'am, he's gone." Five years before, when the doctors had given up hope, Nan and my mother had knelt each side of my father's sickbed and prayed all night—he recovered.

The third movement starts with its muted mini-fugal passages in the strings, allowing the piano to weave arabesques above it: the white seabird of the soul rising from the full swell of the slow movement to circle the stormier waves. Huge moist Irish clouds sail steadily over the liquid outline of the Wicklow hills, while immobile darker clouds offset them lower down the sky. It was Wilhelm Kempff who described the notes in the score of the Fourth Piano Concerto as ravens brooding on their stiff branches. Even at twelve I understood Beethoven's defiant urgency, which reflected huge social tensions as well as his growing deafness. On the morning of my next birthday I woke up to sense a faintly glowing presence in the room: on top of my parents' gift of a new gramophone was a striding statuette of the composer, who took his place among school cups and shields and the cowbells, cuckoo clocks, musical boxes, and little round caps decorated with mountain flowers I had acquired on our Swiss holiday.

My father had sent my mother and three of us siblings to Switzerland in 1951, knowing what a strain it was for her to maintain a constant vigil over his health and ours even in calmer times. In the same year that Nan and my mother had prayed him into recovery, my father put a bet of one pound on an Irish horse called Cahoo in the Aintree Grand National. The odds of a hundred to one were like an unspoken reflection of his survival. The horse romped home; Dublin pubs hardly closed for a week, and my father sent Nan on a shopping spree to London. Thanks to my mother's and Nan's heroic efforts to keep things as normal as possible, I remember little of those years but laughter: "He had me in a black knot laughing." Now, as the slow movement of another Piano Concerto plays, I see my father's coffin being carried down the stairs, and the hearse smothered in flowers slowly passing up the drive carrying my childhood with it. Nan had dressed him and Bartle had shaved him; I often wonder if I should have gone up to say goodbye to the body; but I wanted to keep the memory of my departure back to school on a Sunday evening a month before, when he shook my hand and tumbled several half-crowns into it as reward

90

for a good school report. Of that time, I remember the tenderness, the courtly manners, and the compassion of our staff and neighbours—"I'm sorry for your trouble."

And now my mother is pulling the curtains as the dusk deepens and the branches of the beeches above the wheat-field opposite the window sink into obscurity. The record has finished its scratchy assault through my adolescent emotions and the needle is bopping against the side of the record. My mother, who was to bequeath me the unspoken poetry of her nature, smiles and pours the tea.

9

DREAMING IN AN IMMENSE WORLD

The Irish are sometimes accused of dwelling too much in the past, and indeed much political tension would disappear if the more negative aspects of Irish history were shelved. But this tenacious memory comes in useful these days as Ireland has pressed the Fast Forward button, and the rate of change, alarming everywhere, is positively Heraclitian. Heraclitus, you remember, said that we cannot ever step into the same river twice. In Ireland today, you cannot step into the same history twice, even if that history is literally yesterday. I remember seeing, in 1982, a shop called Here Today—predictably, it had gone by my next visit. Apart from reflecting a perennial modern angst, that shop sign spoke volumes about the state of the country in the early eighties, when Ireland really did get close to going under. Then, to the amazement of the rest of the world, the phenomenon known as The Celtic Tiger picked up steam, so that today Ireland is one of the richest (per capita income) countries in Europe.

As someone who grew up in the "old Ireland" of the 1940s, 1950s, and 1960s, this turnaround is both immensely gratifying and radically disorienting. Few of the traditional landmarks of experience remain. Even a re-visit after a year or two produces experiences that can only be called hallucinatory. This, unfortunately, is reflected in cash-flow terms—houses one remembers from one's youth as nothing to shout about now sell for sums that would have made Paul Getty wince, and keep leaping upwards in price after those two years. Recently, a disused tool-shed in a formerly rundown part of the city went for 220,000 euros. And Dublin, once a shabbily genteel provincial capital whose undeniably beautiful old houses were visibly sagging, has become a traffic-snarled, Armani-suited, go-getting, don't-park-here-or-else modern city. The emerald isle is now the enameled isle, and saints and scholars are not much in evidence. William Blake once wrote: "To generalize is to be an idiot." In Ireland, I am constantly reminded of that wise saying as every idiotic assumption that life will proceed along sane and rational lines is shattered every day.

But the Irish have a long experience in dealing with absurdity and the irrational. There is a story that Samuel Beckett was once mugged and stabbed on a street in Paris; James Joyce went to visit him in hospital; all Beckett was complaining about was the fact that his overcoat was ripped in the affray. Joyce chuckled: "How Irish he is." And mention of these two great writers reminds us that it is perhaps the Irish attitude to language that has kept them, if not always materially successful, at least capable of sanity. The Irish still use language with an Elizabethan relish and panache. A day hardly goes by without overhearing such talk as (of a snobbishly social-climbing lady): "The last time she was anywhere was leaning over a half-door." Or (of a mean person): "He wouldn't give you an itch in case you'd scratch it." Or (of a ruthless business-person): "She'd eat you without salt."

This saltiness and sauciness is meat and drink to the Irish. Added to this is an impish quality in the way the Irish talk and write that prompted Peter Ustinov to compare the Irish and the Russian senses of humour. In a lecture once given in Ireland, Ustinov told with delight of the occasion when he was hopelessly lost somewhere in the depths of the Irish countryside on his way to a reception in his honour. He eventually pulled up beside an old man outside a cottage and asked if he was going in the right direction. After a rambling account of the treachery of the highways and byways of the district, the old man graciously admitted that he was as lost as Ustinov himself. Chuckling, Ustinov drove on, but had hardly gone two hundred yards, when he saw the man wildly signaling in his rear-view mirror. When Ustinov had reversed, the old man informed him with truly surreal relish that he had just had a chat with his brother, "and he doesn't know the way either." Ustinov was laughing all the way to the party (assuming he ever got there).

It is not just the famous Irish way with words. It encapsulates a whole world-view. Ireland remains, for all its recent material success, a country full of a quirkiness and idiosyncrasy that has almost vanished in many other places. I recently asked an inhabitant of New Ross, County Wexford to help me to master the procedures of the new parking regulations. In another verbal dance of several minutes, he did put me on the right track, concluding with: "There you are, now. As handy as a pocket in a shirt." This transformed a tedious bureaucratic procedure into a poetic experience. Through long practice at amusing and bemusing the foreigner, many Irish people have the ability to suddenly absent themselves from practicality awhile, and to start dreaming the immensity of the world into existence (to adapt a phrase of Gaston Bachelard's). It is as if this tiny island, adrift in the rough seas off the edge of Europe, were suddenly aware of itself as anchoring the dizzying drift of the rotating earth—were to become "the still point of the turning world."

Let me illustrate the above observation with what some would call a "senior moment," but which was certainly a memorable one. After I had successfully parked my car in New Ross, I saw a pub called Kennedy's on the corner overlooking the quayside and the river. I went in, and immediately realized how the pub had got its name: portraits of JFK looked down from every wall. The Kennedy ancestral farm is just a few miles away from New Ross, visited by JFK himself in 1963, only months before his assassination. I ordered lunch, which included the best floury potatoes I had had for decades; they were British Queens, said the proprietress proudly. My window seat looked out to the quayside, where a replica of a famine ship was berthed, with American, Canadian, and Irish flags fluttering. I then remembered incongruously that, as a boy, I had cycled around Ireland, and had been stuck for a bed in New Ross, where I spent the night "in jail," the concrete floor of the police station having been put at my disposal. That lunch was one of those occasions when diverse and unconnected material converges into a timeless moment, a still point when contemplation, memory, and imagination mingle. The immensity of experience is arrested in a coming-togetherness, a reflection and a magnifying of the soul. John Fitzgerald Kennedy, famine ship, boyish adventure, British Queens, parking meters: all converged in a moment of metaphorical unity, of hallucination. At such times, one feels at home in the world, in one's own skin, in one's own country past and present, a citizen of an enlarged community of the mind.

In the famous opening of L. P. Hartley's novel, *The Go-Be-tween*, he writes: "The past is a foreign country: they do things differently there." This quotation haunts me whenever I visit Ireland, or even think about it. It is similar to the feeling the traveller gets when the Wicklow Mountains emerge from the sea as the Holyhead ferry approaches Dublin Bay. Or as the plane from London turns north near Arklow over those same mountains, revealing a bird's-eye view of Dublin Bay from Dalkey Island to Howth Castle. Or as the transatlantic plane, having departed from some huge city, coasts in over the Shannon estuary—all Irish people on board becoming strangely silent and brooding—and the plane seems about to land in a cow-and-sheep-sprinkled pasture. It is not only that one is going back in time; rather, it is as if the Irish Tourist Board provided visitors with a time-machine—one is going to slip in and out of various centuries in the course of a visit. The visitor, maybe expecting the postcard or guidebook clichés about old-fashioned charm and blarney, will be greeted initially by a briskly contemporary people whose attitude to the present is both pragmatic and dismissive, as if to say: "Get on with it, but don't bore us with bottom lines and windows of opportunity. Speak your mind and make sure you have a mind to speak."

The Irish mind is as richly layered with voices played off in suspension as any Bach fugue. The seeming linguistic madness of *Finnegans Wake* is not just the product of a warped verbal genius, but comes from that same textured, everyday soil. Every time you look, it's a different country—now you see it, now you don't—and this is reflected in the various languages one is likely to encounter in the course of a day, from colour-supplement newspeak to archaisms: after an attempt to ask directions in County Cork, my sister and I were greeted with "Gorgeous to see ye." Predictably, with the Dublin genius for inventing names, the Millennium Spire in O'Connell Street on the site of the former Nelson's Pillar, blown up and demolished in 1966, is nicknamed "The Stiletto in the Ghetto." And the new Luas (pronounced Lewis) tram system is called the "Daniel Day": "Good luck now, I'm off to catch the Daniel Day."

Trams. Are they making a comeback, along with turntables and Beatles' songs—a sign of our nostalgia for a simpler, more innocent world? Maybe not simpler and more innocent, but certainly slower: I used to lull myself to sleep with the intricate rhythms of the sound of the wheels of the old Howth tram as it clacked its way down the slope from the Summit of the Baily, slowing to stop at the double-line junction just above my parents' garden; then a cacophony of clattering wheels as it crossed the points onto a single line again, rattled down the hill to the Redrock junction, then past the cemetery at Saint Fintan's, stopping opposite the side gate of Howth Castle, and out of hearing down to Sutton Cross. But not out of my imagination or inner ear. *The Irish Times* came sailing over the top of our garden wall every morning as the tram groaned up from Sutton Cross, tossed out of his open platform by Mr. Maypother, the driver. (Rumour had it that Lord Revelstoke's newspaper was dropped onto Lambay Island from a tiny aircraft). What eejit (idiot) in a government office planned the demise of that legendary tram? Coloured navy blue and rich cream, those slow-moving carriages were the gossip-boxes of the neighbourhood; as for the upper deck, open to the elements and passing branches, it was a child's paradise as the tram swayed around the whole Hill of Howth, the dredgers and mail steamers throwing up distant spray from their heaving bows in Dublin Bay below.

Our beloved housekeeper, Nan, was the dynamo that kept much of this shifting, flickering conversation going, with her huge appetite for the quirks of human nature—she was never in short supply of material in the Baily. Every slight infringement of sanity or common sense was picked up by her skeptical radar and relayed to my father, laid up on his sickbed. Just as the local publicans had her Paddy and Red (a lethal mixture of Paddy's whiskey and red lemonade) ready to slide down the bar on her appearance, so the tram-drivers were in amused awe of her imperious progress:

"Maypother, stop that tram and let me get to me work."

"Is that yourself, Nan? Can't you wait until the junction?"

"I'm fallin' outa me stannin' with the work I did yesterday . . . You're stoppin'. You're a grand fella, Maypother. I'll say a word in me prayers for you."

"Nan, you're a caution. I'll be seeing you tomorrow."

"Please God you will. Wait now till I collect me bags. There, I'm down. Gee up, now. God bless, Maypother."

And so the tram of my childhood clattered on its archaic way, out of sight, out of hearing, out of history, but not out of mind. As for Nan, she did not cease from mental fight nor did her sword of wit sleep in her hand until her death in 1989.

The past is a foreign country. Yes, but we still carry the map of that place around, imprinted on the parchment of our brains. Although our passport to that country has long ago expired or been lost, the once-upon-a-timeness of things is strangely present in everything we do, as we attempt to dream ourselves into the immensity of life. These feelings are greatly heightened by change, especially rapid and seemingly ruthless alteration. Such is the experience of returning to the Ireland of the Celtic Tiger. In comforting counterbalance to the Heraclitian flux, I often repeat to myself the old French saying: *"Plus ça change. . ."*— "The more things change, the more they really stay the same."

10

A LITERARY PILGRIM IN EUROPE

One of the favourite books in my collection is *Guide Littéraire de la France*, purchased in Paris in September 1965. On re-reading it recently, I found a review of the *Guide* by Cyril Connolly, cut out of one of the Sunday newspapers that same year. It is entitled "Marcel Proust Slept Here." Connolly applies his legendary erudition to the volume, suggesting all kinds of authors and places omitted; he concludes, however, on a comic note echoing the archness of the title. He wonders why some of us are so obsessed with this kind of pilgrimage, starting usually in pursuit of famous names, and guttering down into trivia about authors known to just the Betjemans of this world. It is like travelling to English houses looking for beds in which Queen Elizabeth I is alleged to have slept. A harmless enough activity, but along the way, an observant pilgrim will pick up a wealth of knowledge.

Pilgrimages, after all, are undertaken with very mixed motives, as we know from reading *The Canterbury Tales*: adventure, curiosity, fresh air, flirting, display, and, perhaps, piety. It is one of the pleasures of my retirement that I have more time to revive my youthful interest in hunting out places associated with great literature. Furthermore, I don't have to justify such expenditure of time to those academics who would regard such wanderings as "amateur" and irrelevant to the serious study of literature. Well, I remain an amateur, as long as I am understood as meaning someone who, while striving for scholarly scrupulousness in my writing and lecturing, also learns a great deal from seeing authors in their habit as they lived (or at least in their habitat). One becomes a kind of field naturalist eager to learn how different environments have produced such diverse species, how a *locus* gets to be a *locus classicus*, how writers are sensitive to the *genius loci*. Or to put it in Darwinian terms, how small changes in geography and weather have an evolutionary effect on works of art as well as on flora and fauna.

Oscar Wilde once quipped that Whistler's paintings of London fogs had made those infamous "pea-soupers" visible for the first time. We all know that people had seen them before, but not, it is implied, in quite the same way. Wilde's insight, as usual, is spot on. Beloved spots in nature have usually been transformed in our imaginations, often through the influence of works of art. What would the French countryside be without Sisley, Pissarro, Monet, and Renoir? In the same way, we see the English landscape through the brushstrokes of John Constable. Painters have taught us to read landscapes, just as novelists have taught us to read character, and poets to read feelings. Our favourite places not only convey a sense of *déjà vu* but of *déjà lu*.

Even as a child, places were poet-haunted for me. I spent my early childhood exploring the cliff-paths and byways of the Howth Peninsula, a promontory celebrated in Gaelic poetry as far back as the sixth century, collected in such works as *The Garland of Howth*. My teens were spent within a mile of The Meeting of the Waters, where the Avonmore glides down from Glenmalure to join the Avonbeg. This symbolic watery joining of forces had been made famous by Thomas Moore in a romantic lyric. Just as actual signposts in the Fen Country point to the village of Clare, Suffolk, the whole landscape points to Clare. Just as the mental street-signs of Dublin say Swift, Beckett, and Joyce, the street-signs of Paris say Villon, Baudelaire, and Prévert. All Warwickshire laneways lead to Shakespeare; every crag in the Lake District shouts Wordsworth; the wheat-fields around Illiers in the Beauce, west of Paris, sway to the rhythms of Proust's long sentences; the area north of Orléans and Tours, with its walled rose gardens, is haunted by Ronsard's love lyrics and sonnets; County Sligo belongs to Yeats; Bordeaux was put on the map by Montaigne and Montesquieu; the flat, marshy country south of Paris, known as La Sologne, is the Lost Domain of Alain-Fournier; the Scottish border country is inseperable from Sir Walter Scott; the pathways over the Wicklow hills echo to the ghostly footsteps of John Millington Synge, accompanied by his dog, Ben. It is not just idyllic landscapes that vibrate with these influences: Philip Larkin has been called "the John Clare of the building sites", and T. S. Eliot is as present in urban wastelands as he is at Little Gidding in Cambridgeshire.

Art digests and absorbs our experience for us, so that our relationships with people and places are subtly transformed. A whole atlas of countries of the mind exists in one's imagination. Sometimes, this leads to radical disillusion: Thomas Gray looks across the water-meadows towards Eton, the intervening distance of space and time irrevocably separating him from his happy childhood—"where ignorance is bliss." Housman similarly looks over the Shropshire landscape towards Ludlow, wondering "What fields, what spires are those?" and concluding that they compose a "land of lost content." But there is triumph also in being a mental traveller. In one of his moving tributes to Lady Gregory, in the short poem "The New Faces," Yeats imagines himself, if she were the first to die, avoiding those places, especially Coole Park, where they had together achieved so much. The poem ends in defiance of time: "Our shadows rove the garden gravel still,/The living seem more shadowy than they." (Finneran 211) Yeats is quite right; the tourists who come today to Coole Park seem insubstantial compared to the powerful spirits of the place, the benign shadows cast by the great men and women who made this place what it is, one of the focal points of modern Irish culture.

So, my imagination was already well stocked when I set out recently to expand my mental atlas. I took the advice of that experienced travel writer, Jan Morris, to confine my searches to a few specific themes. Along with references to art and landscapes, the main theme of this essay is the magnetic hold that places associated with writers have on my imagination.

My first cultural stop was Arundel Castle in West Sussex. This castle has everything to satisfy the most bloodthirsty child—two of the family were executed, there is a realistic mock-up of the castle under siege in the Civil War, a superb drawbridge in working order, and a deep and damp dungeon in the Norman keep where enemies of the family were shoved, "to ponder the error of their ways." The most discriminating tourist will find treasures galore—Van Dyck's portrait of Charles I, a room designed around three superb Canalettos, and so on. Apart from its grandeur, the place has especial historical interest, in that the residents, the Duke of Norfolk and his family, have remained staunch

Catholics throughout over nine centuries of turbulent British history. The family name is Howard, and among a succession of family pictures is a portrait of Henry Howard, Earl of Surrey, a great literary innovator. Howard not only, with Wyatt, brought the Italian sonnet to England but also invented blank verse in his translation of *The Aeneid*—two key moments in English literature. Henry Howard lived mainly at Framlingham Castle, Suffolk, now a ruin, and fell foul of the religious tensions after the Reformation; he was executed by Henry VIII at the age of thirty.

Another literary echo was running through my head as I walked around the estate, especially in the chapel in the grounds where members of the family are buried. In "An Arundel Tomb", Philip Larkin is moved by the Earl and Countess holding each other's hands in stone, how they

> Persisted, linked, through lengths and breadths
> Of time. Snow fell, undated. Light
> Each summer thronged the glass. A bright
> Litter of birdcalls strewed the same
> Bone-riddled ground. And up the paths
> The endless altered people came.
> (Thwaite 116)

And up that path I came, too, eager to read as well as look in a voyeuristic way at all these marvels. I sometimes quote to my students those magical three words: "Snow fell, undated." to demonstrate the powerful compression that poetry at its best achieves. The poem says more than many an historical treatise.

After several days culture-vulturing in London, seeing Handel's harpsichord in Kew Palace, the botanical wonders in

Kew Gardens, the conservatory at Syon House containing the vine from which a cutting was planted in Australia to inaugurate the Australian wine industry, I took the train to Cambridge.

The first time I visited Cambridge as a starry-eyed youth studying literature, I was struck by how many of the major English poets had been educated there. When it comes to science, the place is no slouch, the Cavendish laboratory scientists winning a clutch of Nobel Prizes. At one time, one Cambridge college used to boast that it had won more Nobels than the whole of France. But it is also rich as a seed-bed of literature, especially poetry: Chaucer, Spenser, Milton, George Herbert, Andrew Marvell, Lord Byron, Tennyson, Wordsworth, Coleridge, Rupert Brooke, Ted Hughes, and Sylvia Plath are just the most prominent names. This time, I stayed just two days in Cambridge, and because of an excursion to Ely Cathedral, had time for just four of my favourite colleges: King's, Clare, Trinity, and Saint John's.

Cambridge is smaller and its marvels are more concentrated than Oxford's. The string of colleges along the River Cam with its drifting punts is one of the show-pieces of England. Clare, its delicious scholars' garden providing convenient benches to watch the punts, is Siegfried Sassoon's college. This soldier-poet, born of wealthy parents, spent four years in the trenches, and, with Wilfrid Owen, helped inaugurate the modern poetry of shock and protest. In "The Dug-Out" he shakes a huddled soldier by the shoulder: *"You are too young to fall asleep for ever/And when you sleep you remind me of the dead."* (Sassoon 35)

King's, next door to Clare, is Rupert Brooke's college. Brooke's poems are now dated in the way Sassoon's are not, coming as they do from the other end of the telescope, so to speak, of that long war. Brooke's generation went to the slaughter as if taking part in an old-fashioned cavalry charge. Ironically, Brooke died of an infected mosquito bite early in the war. E. M. Forster was another student at King's, and later was an honorary Fellow. Forster's novels are modern all right, with their sadness and irony. I have two memories of King's: in 1969, I was staying in one of the guest suites, and passed Forster shuffling on his way to dinner. In 1971, I went to evensong at King's: to my delight, it was a special occasion, with the Eton choir as well as the famous King's choir. The service commemorated the 500th anniversary of the death of the founder of Eton and King's, King Henry VI, in 1471. The Provost led the choir up the long aisle, carrying a single red rose—the rose of Lancaster, which is carved in stone all over the cliff-like walls of this Perpendicular masterpiece. Because of the turbulence in Henry's reign, King's Chapel took almost a hundred years to build.

Along Trinity Street, one comes to the massive Tudor gateway into Trinity. On the right of the gate are Newton's rooms, where he lived as a young Fellow of the college, having gone home for eighteen months during the plague and done some sums that changed the world. Vladimir Nabokov came up to Trinity in 1920, after his family had escaped from the Bolshevik Revolution. He occupied "intolerably squalid" rooms in Trinity Lane. Lord Byron published his first book of poems while an undergraduate here, in between falling in love with a choir-boy in the chapel, and keeping a tame bear. Since dogs were not allowed in the college, the aristocratic youth had to go one better. Another eccentric poet who became a Lord, Tennyson, studied here, as did Arthur Hallam, whose death moved Tennyson to write one of the great poems of the nineteenth century, "In Memoriam":

But, for the unquiet heart and brain,
A use in measured language lies;
The sad mechanic exercise,
Like dull narcotics, numbing pain.

In words, like weeds, I'll wrap me o'er,
Like coarsest clothes against the cold;
But that large grief which these enfold
Is given in outline and no more.
(Abrams et al. vol. 2, 1088)

There was madness in Tennyson's family; his huge output as a poet was a kind of narcotic escape, a "sad mechanic exercise." He knew only too well the truth of Shakespeare's lines: "The lunatic, the lover, and the poet/Are of imagination all compact . . ." All three types are out of their minds.

The choir was throwing echoes around the superb acoustics of the chapel at Saint John's, Wordsworth's college, when I entered. Although Wordsworth once struck a portrait in his father's house with a whip, seemingly forecasting instability, he was very much the earnest youth as he trundled south in the coach, as he describes it in *The Prelude*, catching an excited glimpse of the pinnacles of King's, across Magdelene Bridge, and up to the door of his inn, the Hoop. After the "first glitter of the show" had worn off, Wordsworth makes an astonishing decision (and a risky one for somebody expected by his family to become a don, a lawyer, or a cleric). He decides he is not cut out for relentless academic pursuits, and he writes:

But wherefore be cast down,
Why should I grieve?—I was a chosen Son.
For hither had I come with holy powers

And faculties, whether to work or feel:
To apprehend all passions and all moods
Which time, and place, and season do impress
Upon the visible universe, and work
Like changes there by force of my own mind.
(Jonathan Wordsworth et al. 96)

Against the full might of the University of Cambridge, Wordsworth pits his mountainy instinct that he will trust his own feelings and insights to educate himself. Romantic, indeed.

Eager to see for myself the landscape that had inspired Wordsworth to such foolhardy beliefs, I took the train from Cambridge to Lancaster. We proceeded at a fair lick through Middle England: Cambridgeshire, Rutland, and on via Birmingham to Lancashire. We passed the outer fringes of John Clare country, a landscape I have walked, driven, and cycled through many times. It is an undramatic countryside, perhaps more essentially English in its reticence than the rough-edged Lake District. It contains much of interest: Peterborough and Ely Cathedrals, the latter one of the most impressive of all medieval buildings; and an almost perfectly preserved Georgian market town, Stamford, where *Middlemarch* was filmed. Outside Stamford is the Elizabethan extravaganza of Burghley House, where Clare was a gardener for a while. The Northamptonshire churches have tall slender spires unlike any others in England, and, over all, those huge East Anglian skies so beloved of Constable.

My cousin was waiting at Lancaster station for me. We drove north for an hour, then the terrain changed: hilly, twisty roads, deserted moorland, with the local breed of sheep— Herdwicks—sleeping on the warm pavement, unconcerned at the car weaving between them. When Geoffrey started opening and closing gates, I knew we were close to home. After the sixth gate, he said, "This is my farm, Whincop; you'll see it in the morning." We pulled into a large court-yard with a heavy wind thrashing in the old farmyard trees, into a cosy thick-walled kitchen, where Geoffrey produced a hot stew, and on into a sitting-room where he soon had a blazing log fire going. After demolishing a bottle of wine, we retired to that thick-eyed deep sleep you only get in remote regions.

In the morning, Geoffrey asked: "Would you like a bath?" I accepted and went on my way. It was while absentmindedly brushing my teeth that I looked up, out the newly double-glazed and enlarged window, and immediately knew why Wordsworth had taken on Cambridge. I have seen the Alps, I have seen the Rockies, I have—you name it—but I would "need colours and forms that are unknown to man" to describe the scene. In the middle distance was the Esk Valley, a river of green dotted with the occasional white farmhouse; beyond rose Skiddaw and other mountains, fold upon fold. I realised also that Wordsworth had got the measure of this country better than any painter, and passages of his work rose spontaneously to my mind:

> Magnificent
> The morning was, a memorable pomp,
> More glorious than I ever had beheld.
> The sea was laughing at a distance; all
> The solid mountains were as bright as clouds,
> Grain-tinctured, drenched in empyrean light;
> And in the meadows and the lower grounds
> Was all the sweetness of a common dawn.
> (Jonathan Wordsworth et al. 142)

After that dawn, which was also the dawn of Romanticism in England, Wordsworth was on his way, finding books in the running brooks and sermons in stones.

On the first day of my visit, we went hiking. On the second day, Geoffrey drove me up the Esk Valley to Grasmere, where he had arranged for the Director of the Wordsworth Trust to greet us and show us around. Knowing of my work on Clare, the Director showed us books with Clare's signature, first editions, paintings, and other treasures of the Wordsworth Museum and the new Jerpoint Centre—together the greatest resource in the world for scholars of British Romanticism. He then gave us a free ticket to Dove Cottage and garden, restored as far as possible to how it was when Wordsworth and Dorothy lived here (1799-1808). The Wordsworth Trust was founded in 1890, immediately securing Dove Cottage "for the eternal possession of those who love English poetry all over the world." The literary vibrations are tangible; one almost expects Coleridge to enter after one of his long rambles—Coleridge, like William and Dorothy, was a prodigious walker. Dorothy jots in her journal for 29 August 1800: "At 11 o'clock Coleridge came . . . over Helvellyn—Wm was gone to bed and John also. We sate and chatted till past three W. in his dressing gown. Coleridge read us a part of Christabel."

The next day we drove up the Duddon Valley, the river Wordsworth had traced to its source as a youth, and about which he wrote the *River Duddon* sequence of sonnets: "Still glides the stream, and shall for ever glide."

If the Lake District belongs imaginatively to Wordsworth, thousands of acres of it used to literally belong to Beatrix Potter, bequeathed by her to the National Trust, including several large working farms and her house, Hill Top, in Near Sawrey. Since the publication of *Peter Rabbit* in 1901, millions of the world's children have enjoyed her delicate watercolours, many of them set in and around her home. One of the guides in Hill Top was a Japanese woman; the Japanese are as devoted to Potter as they are to Lucy Maud Montgomery. Once again, Potter's imagination suffuses the place; no great novelist or poet has had more of an impact on a specific landscape. As a child, I remember staring fascinated at Potter's drawings of curly cabbages; here they were in the garden. Which was more real, this or that?

On to the shores of Coniston Water, where a huge pile on the hillside declared itself to be Brantwood House, the home for twenty-eight years of John Ruskin. Ruskin was one of those great Victorians who achieved in one lifetime enough for six people. In the late nineteenth century, he was regarded as a sage and prophet, and Brantwood was an intellectual power-house. According to Kenneth Clark, he was the best watercolourist of the second half of the nineteenth century (the first half was dominated by Turner, whom Ruskin had championed). Tolstoy described Ruskin as "one of those rare men who think with their hearts, and so he thought and said not only what he himself had seen and felt, but what everyone will think and say in the future."

In 1904, a young Indian lawyer took Ruskin's "Unto This Last" on a long train journey. So impressed was he by this "great book" that he "determined to change his life in the light of this book." The lawyer became Mahatma Gandhi. Others who were deeply influenced by Ruskin were William Morris and Marcel Proust. His writings on conservation led directly to the work of the National Trust, a body which maintains and protects hundreds of historic places, homes, and landscapes. Canon Rawnsley, one of the founders, wrote: "It was Ruskin's teaching which was the fountain head of the teaching which set forward this National Trust." In an astonishing essay, "The Storm-cloud of the Nineteenth Century", Ruskin predicted what we now call the "greenhouse effect"; he continually warned readers about the baleful results of unrestrained industrial activity, which produced "blanched sun" . . . "blighted grass" . . . and "blinded man." An excellent video in the house covered all these topics, and a restaurant on the terrace provided superb views across Coniston Water to the Old Man of Coniston and adjacent mountains.

Before dropping me off at Liverpool airport, from where I flew to Geneva, Geoffrey took a side road in mid-Lancashire to show me Hoghton Tower, home of the de Hoghton family, still Catholic. Contemporary Shakespeare scholars believe that Shakespeare was tutor to this family during his "lost" years, from his late teens until he went to London and started making his name. Scholars believe that Shakespeare, while outwardly conformist, maintained secret sympathies with the Old Faith, and was a relatively safe bet for the family to harbour at a time when Queen Elizabeth's spies were combing the country looking for outlawed Catholic practices. If this is true, it gave the dramatist early experience of people who knew how to be "lords and owners of their faces."

And so to Geneva, where my niece collected me, accompanied by a friend, Alain, who acts as her chauffeur. My sister had flown out from Dublin two days before. Alain was at our fortunate disposal throughout our visit. My niece works in Geneva and lives in the small town of Ferney-Voltaire a few miles on the French side of the city. Voltaire bought the château at Ferney at the height of his fame—he was far enough from Paris to avoid, for the most part, any trouble with the French *ancien régime*. No less an artist than David sculpted the statue in the town celebrating "*le patriarche de Ferney.*"

Next day, Alain drove us to the old quarter of Geneva. We wandered the steep cobbled streets, found the house where Borges used to live, and had lunch opposite an imposing house—the birthplace of Jean-Jacques Rousseau. The ample first floor was devoted to an excellent permanent exhibition of Rousseau's life and work. I had recently re-read *The Confessions*, one of the oddest and most unintentionally funny books ever written. Rousseau himself was as odd as a bag of cats, but a born writer, and one of the most influential figures of the past two hundred and fifty years. He fell out with almost everybody, including Voltaire—a formidable enemy—and retained no great love for his native country. The inhabitants of a Swiss village once pelted him with stones. It is not every writer who can claim to have been stoned out of their own country (although Beckett once said that working for the French Resistance was easier on his nerves than living in Ireland). One of Rousseau's friends later inspected the site of the fray, exclaiming "My God, it's a quarry!"

The second day of our visit, Alain drove us through the lovely region of Haute Savoie (an important centre of French resistance) to the picturesque town of Annecy, with its own lake, smaller and prettier than Lake Geneva. It was in Annecy that Rousseau met Madame de Warens, one of those aristocratic women who protected this strange man much in need of mothering and protection. He lived at her estate further south at Chambéry—Les Charmettes—for five years, an idyllic time in his life. Rousseau, like Wordsworth, fell in love with Nature; between them, they changed the modern sensibility, and "invented" mountain scenery. Again, like Wordsworth, Rousseau was a constant walker, an activity that stimulated them both to creativity. As he puts it in *The Confessions*: "When I stay in one place I can hardly think at all; my body has to be on the move to set my mind going." (158)

One of the delights of travel for an Irish expatriate is the likelihood of finding an Irish pub in the vicinity. My sister and I counted at least five. One of them is a favourite with my niece, and we met many of her friends and colleagues there. It was during a lively conversation about Irish writers with Bodhan, a Ukrainian working for the UN, that he asked me to take part in a one-day conference to commemorate the Ukrainian/Russian writer, Gogol's, visit to Ferney in 1836. On the third day of our visit, we assembled at the gate of Le Château de Voltaire, where we were to get a special viewing of the house. An eloquent woman spoke first about Voltaire's life and work, especially his impact on the town of Ferney. After photographic sessions, we were given a tour of the interior of the château. Here were the rooms in which the great man entertained a host of people from every walk of life. It was here also that he sheltered the Calas family, Protestant victims of religious fanaticism. This supremely gifted man, the epitome of the eighteenth-century Enlightenment, had spent two spells in the Bastille, and had lived for some years in England, whose liberalism he admired. (Knowledgeable about Newtonian physics, he attended Newton's funeral in Westminster Abbey in 1727, and irritated the French by his Anglophile attitudes—"See, in England, a scientist gets the funeral of a King.") He had also worked for Frederick the Great in Berlin. On the wall of the salon at Ferney, there is a simple inscription: *Son esprit est partout, mais son coeur est ici.* ("His spirit is everywhere, but his heart is here").

That evening, there was a series of talks in the courtyard of a local bookshop in Ferney town, with a good attendance. Bodhan reminded us that, as well as Gogol a hundred and seventy years ago that day, Lord Byron had visited Ferney on that date in 1816, both of them paying homage to the memory of *le patriarche de Ferney*. I reminded the audience in my talk that Byron had written of himself in *Don Juan* as "The grand Napoleon of the realms of rhyme." (McGann 734). Later that evening, there was a reception in the Town Hall, the Mayor graciously presenting me with a handsome book on the town and Voltaire's involvement with the people. I gave another talk, stressing how such Irish writers as Yeats, Synge, George Moore, Beckett, and Joyce had regarded French literature and Paris as an essential point in a triangle—comprising Dublin, London, Paris—which enabled them to transcend the usually acerbic see-saw between Ireland and England. The theme of the conference was how Gogol, coming from provincial Russia, had become a central figure in Russian literature. I finished with a quotation from Oscar Wilde, which, in his usual fashion, wittily drew attention to the gains in this process as well as the losses. Wilde was once asked in Paris why he did not speak the ancient language of Ireland—Gaelic. He replied: "Sir, I am an Irishman, that is to say, one condemned to speak the language of Shakespeare."

The next day, Alain drove us along the north shore of Lake Geneva to Vevey, the hills of the west end of the lake changing into vistas of Alpine grandeur to the east. My sister had a long search, eventually successful, for cuckoo clocks, once ubiquitous in Switzerland. We had the local delicacy, *perche à l'orange*, at a restaurant on the square, and I knew why Charlie Chaplin and my favourite actress—Audrey Hepburn—had settled nearby. We then took a boat trip on the lake, passing the pebbly beach where we had swum on a family holiday in 1951. At the east end of the lake sits the brooding Château de Chillon. Byron was here also on his visit, and wrote several poems on the release of a political prisoner from its notorious dungeons (a good deal damper than Arundel's, as the château almost floats on the lake):

> Chillon! Thy prison is a holy place,
> And thy sad floor an altar—for 'twas trod,
> Until his very steps have left a trace
> Worn, as if thy cold pavement were a sod,
> By Bonnivard! May none those marks efface!
> For they appeal from tyranny to God.
> (Perkins, *Romantic Writers*, 793)

I remember those dungeons from the 1951 trip, when, as a carefree boy, such things were picturesque rather than tragic.

Then it was time to move on. After much hugging of my niece's cat and dog, we flew from Geneva to Dublin. A few days later, I drove to West Cork, stopping along the way in Castletownshend, a tiny seaside village immortalised by Edith Somerville, author, with her cousin Martin Ross, of *Experiences of an Irish R.M.* These brilliant writers are sometimes mistakenly regarded as writing about Irish local characters from the outside, from the perspective of genteel ladies of the Protestant gentry. Nobody has ever written more evocatively of country pursuits, especially hunting. Edith wrote, painted, played the organ in the local church, and was Master of the West Carbery Hunt. The following letters from neighbours show that, far from disapproving of hunting, the local people were in league with Edith when it came to the depredations of foxes. The letters also demonstrate that the "picturesque" language that Somerville and Ross are sometimes accused of inventing was part and parcel of their immediate existence:

"Dear Miss, just a few lines to let you know the fox is making a great set on me I am beggared with him he have 8 hens and 2 ducks carried and I badly in want of them. Excuse me for making so stiff I remain your truly Mrs Cotter."

"I thought I had the house well fastened but he scrope under the door. . . . every wet night always we finds his foot marks around the fowl house we found them in the fields around partly eaten and wasn't it a terrible loss to any poor young woman . . . when ye will come the way here after, we will do all in our power for ye to help ye to catch him." (Lewis 126)

After a month's stay in West Cork, I drove north via Killaloe to County Mayo. Just south of Galway city is the small village of Gort, outside which is the entrance to Coole Park, now looked after by the Office of Public Works. I have several times in the past paid my respects to Lady Gregory's memory; this time I had to pass by with the ghosts of her famous visitors in my mind's eye.

I stayed for two days with friends near Ballinrobe on the shores of Lough Carra. A short walk away is the romantic ruin of Moore Hall, once home of George Moore. On an island in the lake are scattered his ashes: "There is a lake in every man's heart . . ." as he writes in *The Lake*. Moore Hall, like Coole Park, is suffused with that wistful, tragic atmosphere created by the twists and turns of Irish history. Although the family was Catholic, the house was burnt down in "The Troubles." A plaque now reads nearby:

"Burial place of the Moores of Moore Hall. This Catholic patriot family is honoured for their famine relief and their refusal to barter principles for English gold. Erected by Ballyglass Coy. Old IRA 1964."

On my way through the Midlands, I passed through Edgeworthstown, home of Maria Edgeworth, author of *Castle Rackrent* (1800), a novel admired in Russia, especially by Turgenev. And so back to Joyce's "dear, dirty Dublin." My sister and I drove out to the "Lovely Hill of Delightful Howth", as one ancient Irish manuscript describes it. The cliff paths, along which Yeats had walked with Maud Gonne, remained the same as when I first started exploring them about 1947:

> Before I'd read Blake or Dante
> I scribbled my own Mundane Comedy:
> Here be jagged rocks, there a treacherous slope,
> Here a stark lighthouse, there bramble-roofed snugs;
> The Summit reached was a proud achievement.
> Auguries of Experience indeed!

Michael Longley, the Belfast poet, who was a contemporary of mine at Trinity, and whose early work Rivers Carew and I often published in *The Dublin Magazine* in the sixties, launched his *Collected Poems* in Dublin while I was there. I was happy to toast the publication of this impressive volume, fruits of over forty-five years of song-smithing. As one review puts it, Longley's poems have "perfect pitch in troubled times."

Longley, along with half a dozen others at the time, had shown unusual literary promise as an undergraduate. I remember, as co-editor of *The Dublin Magazine*, receiving the accomplished poem "The Hebrides" (*Collected Poems* 22-5), from whose fifth section I quote below:

> Granting the trawlers far below their stance,
> Their anchorage,
> I fight all the way for balance—
> In the mountain's shadow
> Losing foothold, covet the privilege
> Of vertigo.

As a fitting conclusion to my wanderings, I went with a friend to the National Library, its spiky railings reminiscent of scenes in *A Portrait of the Artist as a Young Man,* to see the Yeats Exhibition. This is the most attractively laid-out and displayed exhibition I have ever seen, and worthy of its great subject and his family, Ireland's pre-eminent cultural family. The exhibition will run for three years, a very sensible arrangement, as it gives visitors a chance to make repeated forays into this thickly layered life, one of the central artistic careers of the twentieth century. All around the larger display room are little rooms, like the side-chapels in a cathedral, each with a different theme—all of them illustrating the diverse, surprising facets of this haunting genius—great reckonings in a little room. Among the recorded voices reading selections of the poetry is that of Seamus Heaney appropriately reading "What Then?" by Yeats: "His chosen comrades thought at school/He must grow a famous man." (Finneran 302)

Heaney has himself grown a famous man, who has given poetry a public presence not seen since the time of Tennyson. Unlike some other well-known poets, Heaney's public persona is humble, professional, and dignified, making him a worthy inheritor of that great tradition. Tennyson, however, wrote at a time when the tide of intellectual and artistic endeavour flowed strong, the swell of the Renaissance still washing the shores, in spite of Matthew Arnold's misgivings in "Dover Beach." Yeats in "The Nineteenth Century and After" chronicles the retreat of that tide:

> Though the great song return no more
> There's keen delight in what we have:
> The rattle of pebbles on the shore
> Under the receding wave.
> (Finneran 240)

11

ONLY CONNECT

The tapestry of the Romantic period is vast, so vast that it is perhaps impossible to find a wall anywhere, even in one's mind, big enough to contain it. I am reminded of the history of one Old Master painting: it was cut into many pieces and dispersed around the globe. Art historians have to date traced all but one segment of the painting, and the curators of the National Gallery, London (the owners of the central fragment) have paid handsomely to retrieve the missing parts, so visitors can now see an almost complete picture. The Director of the National Gallery recently announced on television: "If anyone knows the whereabouts of this remaining fragment, we would be most interested in hearing about it." Teachers and scholars of Romanticism seem to be always making a similar request (or re-quest): if anyone out there finds the missing piece of the great jig-saw puzzle called Romanticism, please get in touch immediately. We seem to be permanently out of touch with the subject. Romanticism often works by the method patented by Polonius in *Hamlet*: "by indirections find directions out" (2. 1. 65). Maybe we should not want the missing piece of the painting to be restored; its absence teases us out of thought as doth eternity. To put it in other words, Romanticism is a quest for wholeness that can never be completely achieved or satisfied: fragmentation and frustration are constant companions, which I believe only increases its relevance and importance.

The great Romantics, for all their strong and idiosyncratic personalities, were basically humble in front of the givens of existence. Their language feels its way into perceived truths, rather than assaulting them with the battering rams of logic or the unearned certainties of abstract jargon. What needs to be restored, and there is every sign that it is slowly being restored, is intuition along with tuition, the touch described by Pope in "An Essay on Man": "The spider's touch, so exquisitely fine!/ Feels at each thread, and lives along the line" (Butt 512). The huge task awaiting contemporary critics is the perennial one of absorbing one's predecessors, re-experiencing the original works in all their nakedness, and living along the line with an informed but humble analysis. I use the word "nakedness" advisedly, as it seems that many works have been clothed with so many interpretations, or varnished with so many layers, that one of our first tasks is to patiently clean the canvas, restore the original colours, and discard the fashionable vestments of thought with which they have become encrusted. A. N. Whitehead once complained about the second-handedness of academic thought; today, thought is likely to have been more extensively shop-soiled.

The Romantics had a similar task of renovation two hundred-odd years ago. They inherited a mechanistic language from the eighteenth century, which, in their different ways, they set out to transform. Wordsworth's Preface to *Lyrical Ballads* is still a clarion call to exalted but pragmatic common sense. We need a similar revolution of the wheel of language to restore the place of each spoke in the economy of the circle, radiating outwards from a luminous hub of meaning. If the intellectual master-theme of the Enlightenment was Descartes' "I think, therefore I am", and Rousseau's reaction could be summed up as "I feel, therefore I am", the motto of the true Romantic teacher/scholar should be "I inter-relate, therefore I am." Too much has been made of the Romantic stress on solitude and a corresponding solipsism and "mystification"; the Romantics were also obsessed with community; the fact that few of them achieved satisfactory communal relationships while longing for a true community—Wordsworth's "Perfect Contentment, Unity entire" (Hayden I, 701)—is another way of saying how modern they are.

In my experience, students in the past ten years have become increasingly disenchanted with some of the intellectual orthodoxies of the past thirty years. Although they don't always have the language to articulate it, they are saying: "Yes, there was a lot of dirty water to empty from the bath, but where has the baby gone?" I hope I will not be perceived as flippant in using this homely metaphor, as it reminds me of the Romantic watch-cry: "Back to Nature." These simple slogans are dangerously intoxicating, as the Romantic generation found out, but they contain a multitude of complex attitudes. So, let me make a start in defining what I perceive it entails to be a teacher of Romanticism in 2005 trying to restore the baby, or to get back to nature. I want to concentrate on three areas: avoidance of jargon; a restoration of orality; and a revival of sensuousness. I believe these three areas are inter-connected, and are highlighted by an awareness of ecological principles: the first returns us to linguistic origins; the second returns us to oral immediacy; and the third returns us to the physical.

First, jargon. Two types of jargon should be distinguished:

123

1) the language of specialties and technicalities within any discipline, which practitioners will recognize and non-specialists can learn, given some research; 2) the use of specialized language out of context, or in such a way as to obfuscate the issues and intimidate the reader, often expressed in long, abstract, and ugly words. Orwell's 1947 essay "Politics and the English Language" diagnosed the disease, but his insights have become more and more relevant with each decade. William Zinsser sums up this issue with admirable clarity: ". . . no one who has something original or important to say will willingly run the risk of being misunderstood; people who write obscurely are either unskilled in writing or up to mischief." (62-3). One could add an adaptation of Keats's remark about poetry: "We hate [writing] that has a palpable design upon us." (Wu 1021). Much of the criticism of Romanticism over the past thirty years has had very palpable designs on us, and whether the writers were up to mischief or not, they are often obscure. One of the first tasks of the teacher in the field, therefore, is to point out the difference between the types of jargon outlined above. Most students nowadays read little enough, after all, so we should be alert to guiding them towards the bracing complexity of good scholarship and away from the opaque inertness of vague or pretentious writing. The principles of feng shui, that everything has a field of energy, surely applies to words as well: good writing is full of energy, it generates the electricity of meaning. Bad writing blocks the energy flows of thought, creating a toxic build-up.

Aggressive language seems to sweep all before it in majestic generalizations. Academics have their "buzzwords" as much as any other group. Buzzwords immediately separate the sheep from the goats, the "us" from the "them"; they seem to say, are you a paid-up member in our club? Academics are particularly adept at playing this game, forgetting that the country of knowledge is the birthright of every intelligent being, not the province of self-selecting illuminati. When Wordsworth wrote about wanting to return to the language really used by men, I believe he had in mind something analogous to the situation described by Daniel Nettle and Suzanne Romaine in *Vanishing Voices: the Extinction of the World's Languages*. The authors present a powerful thesis to show that biodiversity has always been linked to linguistic diversity: "Traditional fishermen, particularly on small islands (in Micronesia) where the people still depend on the sea for most of their food, are still rich sources of information unknown to western scientists." (72) This vastly intricate knowledge is internalized and memorized:

"The tides are also timed in relation to lunar phases, and these too were committed to memory. Most of the languages and dialects have specific terms for the paired currents which form on either side of the islands, a region in which these currents converge downstream, and a back current flowing toward the island from this convergence point. The islanders were using their knowledge of current patterns in both fishing and navigation long before they were documented by oceanographers." (Nettle and Romaine 75)

Wordsworth, in admiring the linguistic richness and biodiversity of the Lake District, is tuning in to frequencies that, once silenced, can never return. During the recent outbreak of foot-and-mouth disease in England, there was great concern in the Lake District that the ancient breed of fell sheep would be infected. If so, the instinctive knowledge of thousands of years would be lost, as those sheep are famous for knowing their boundaries without any fences. The internalized knowledge of many peoples whose habitat is at risk

125

has a comparable vulnerability, not just to disease, but to the juggernauts of modernization, allied with the arrogant certainties of the trained experts.

In her 1977 book, *The Ecology of Imagination in Childhood*, (whose very title contains three of the key words in this area), Edith Cobb laments the lack of mutuality in the language of scholarship in her time:

"Unfortunately, the language of conquest still maintains a supreme hold on our social and political theory, our medical policies, and most serious of all, our teaching of ideas about nature and man. Even among naturalists and biologists the realization that in ecology as a biological science we have, for the first time in the history of thought, an instrument for the study of reciprocity and mutuality among categories of thought, as well as among divisions and levels in nature, seems strangely lacking." (24)

Much of the ensuing "discourse" of the final decades of the twentieth century intensified this lack, for all its protestations of "multiculturalism," most of it showing little awareness of, even a contempt for, the kind of humble precision that Cobb describes.

Richness of language accompanies variety of occupation. When one is eroded, the other is impoverished. The diminishment of Gaelic in Ireland followed the decay of traditional crafts and the obliteration of much of the flora and fauna, as explained by Desmond Fennell in "The Last Years of the Gaeltacht" (1981):

"The Gaelic which is spoken today in the Gaeltacht, and which is gradually being abandoned, is a very thin language compared with the spoken Gaelic of three hundred, a hundred, or fifty years ago. . . . a huge loss of vocabulary occurred when the craft industries largely disappeared from the countryside in face of competition from factory products . . . today you see people working in the fields, fishing, gathering seaweed, building houses and making boats. Eighty years ago there were coopers, nail-makers, sail-makers, weavers, tailors, cobblers, and so on. . . ." (qtd. in Foster 442)

These languages are idiomatic and full of the vivid particulars of a way of life, just as the voices of these people are distinctive and individual. Jargon, on the other hand, strings together ready-made thoughts. Under the guise of profound meaning, it delivers a stale monotony rather than the freshness of perception admired by Wordsworth in the Lake District:

". . . because in that condition the passions of men are incorporated with the beautiful and permanent forms of nature. . . .The language, too, of these men is adopted . . . because such men hourly communicate with the best objects from which the best part of language is originally derived . . ." (Wu 357)

Although Wordsworth and Blake approach nature from very different perspectives, Wordsworth in such passages is close to the Blake who wrote: "To Generalize is to be an Idiot. To Particularize is the Alone Distinction of Merit." (Johnson and Grant 440). The Greeks have an expression pointing up a similar contrast: "the poet or the idiot" (Kirkpatrick 532). In other words, if one does not have a touch of the poet, seeking the universal in tiny details, one is likely to string generalities together, losing sight of the roots of meaning. Wordsworth's "spots of time" (Wu 307), Dorothy Wordsworth's incomparable descriptions of the "simplicity, unity, and life" of her environment (Wu 434), Coleridge's acutely observed nature notes— "A dunghill at a distance sometimes smells like musk, and a dead dog like elder-flowers" (Hudson 24)—Byron's flippant down-to-earthness: "And so, for god sake, hock and soda water" (Wu 807), Keats's evocation of the "Season of mists" by making us see and hear "the small gnats" mourning "among the river sallows" (Wu 1080), and Clare's teeming universe of outer and inner weathers—all these are part of the Romantic revolt against what I have called aggressive abstractions.

The French historian, Hippolyte Taine, in his description of Robespierre's use (or misuse) of language, strikes a contemporary disenchanted note. Robespierre, according to Taine, has a ". . . hollow, inflated mind that, filled with words and imagining that these are ideas, revels in its own declamation and dupes itself that it may dictate to others. . . . It might be said he never saw anything with his own eyes, that he neither could nor would see, that false conceptions have intervened and fixed themselves between him and the object; he combines these in logical sequences, and simulates the absent thought by an affected jargon." (McFarland 137-8)

This is strikingly similar to Orwell's diagnosis in 1947:

"The writer [of jargon] either has a meaning and cannot express it, or he inadvertently says something else, or he is almost indifferent as to whether his words mean anything or not. This mixture of vagueness and sheer incompetence is the most marked characteristic of modern English prose, and especially of any kind of political writing. As soon as any topics are raised, the concrete melts into the abstract and no one seems able to think of turns of speech that are not hackneyed: prose consists less and less of words chosen for the sake of their meaning, and more and more of phrases tacked together like the sections of a prefabricated hen-house." (Stubbs and Barnet 267)

Northrop Frye once wrote about a "high authority in the field" of education, whom he describes as "fluent without being articulate." He "cannot break out of an armour of ready-made phrases when he tries to express his real convictions. Once again, nothing can now be done for him: there are no courses in remedial metaphor." (www.mrbauld. com/fryepoet.html).

One of the most productive areas of recent scholarship in the Romantic field has been the turn towards an ecological criticism, by scholars such as Jonathan Bate and James McKusick. A further fruitful development is the return to the extensive quotation of original texts, epitomized by the criticism of Thomas McFarland. And in *The Gang*, John Worthen effectively counters the too-easy assumption that the Romantics worked in solipsistic isolation. These approaches enable one to escape the twin boxes of left-wing or right-wing ideologies, or of old-fashioned humanist versus avant-garde theorist, and find one's bearings in "a language that is ever green" (Bate, "I AM", 147), a line of Clare's that characterizes the new approach. Clare's work especially disproves the contention of some recent critics that the immersion in nature entails a retreat from, or falsification of, political awareness. The political issues shift into what McKusick calls "a zone of ecological conflict" (McKusick 226). For ecocritical scholars, the contemporary relevance of the Romantics, in every sense including the political, is precisely their passionate awareness of the inter-connectedness of natural and human phenomena. The Romantics knew and exemplified the paradox of returning to the origins (and therefore seeming to be archaic) in order to be original. They were, in Kant's phrase, the "favourites of Nature" (Gadamer 21). In discussing Clare as "an increasingly influential model for the current generation of ecological writers," McKusick writes:

"Clare's historical priority in generating a poetic ecolect suggests that modern ecological consciousness did not emerge gradually from an antecedent configuration of scientific concepts, but constitutes a radically new conceptual paradigm that demands a distinctive form of expression." (245, 243)

Contemporary critics espousing an ecological approach are creating "a radically new conceptual paradigm" to restore the origins. They are thus enacting the Romantic quest themselves, by indirections finding directions out.

Another way that teachers and critics of Romanticism can anchor their material in the specific is to remember the connections between literacy and orality. The real language of men is colloquial, idiomatic utterance. It is essentially anecdotal. The word anecdote comes from a Latin stem meaning unpublished material, usually of a personal nature. The pressure of "publish or perish" for professional academics has been so pronounced in recent decades that many scholars have eschewed anecdotal material as unprofessional. The great Romantics, of course, had no such qualms. That sublime egotist, Wordsworth, was steeped in Rousseau, who led the way in substituting the confessional (the personal, emotion-driven) for the professional (the impersonal, fact-driven). This confessional tradition, of course, can lead to triviality and excess, but part of the greatness of the Romantics is their ability to blend the personal with the impersonal. It is not unconnected that many of them were prolific talkers. Coleridge's talk was legendary, and his notebooks often read like overflow conversations (or monologues). Wordsworth, while not possessing the gift of the gab like Coleridge, nevertheless had a very distinctive utterance; who can forget Hazlitt's description of Wordsworth's voice: "a deep guttural intonation, and a strong tincture of the northern *burr*, like the crust on wine."? (Wu 607) And Benjamin Robert Haydon describes "Wordsworth repeating Milton with an intonation like the funeral bell of St Paul's and the music of Handel mingled . . ." (Wu 660) at the "immortal dinner" of 28 December, 1817. Byron, especially in *Don Juan*, catches the idiomatic immediacy of colloquial conversation at all levels of society. And the reader of Keats's letters regrets not to have heard those searing asides as part of the poet's social conversation.

If the printed word is allied to the linear and the eye, the spoken word is intuitive and auditory. Walter J. Ong writes:

"By contrast with vision, the dissecting sense, sound is thus a unifying sense. A typical visual ideal is clarity and distinctness, a taking apart (Descartes' campaigning for clarity and distinctness registered an intensification of vision in the human sensorium). The auditory ideal, by contrast, is harmony, a putting together." (72)

And Ong could be describing the Romantic enterprise in the following: "Knowledge is ultimately not a fractioning but a unifying phenomenon, a striving for harmony. Without harmony, as interior condition, the psyche is in bad health." (72)

The importance of the auditory to Wordsworth is well known. In fact, for a poem ostensibly so much about seeing, "Tintern Abbey" starts with auditory memories:

> Five years have past; five summers, with the length
> Of five long winters! And again I hear
> These waters, rolling from their mountain springs
> With a soft inland murmur.
> (Wu 265)

To see into the life of things is to engage in a unified sensuous response, in touch with the ancient rhythms of nature, and modified by the imagination.

In a defining Romantic gesture, Wordsworth read the completed *Prelude* aloud to Coleridge and others at Coleorton Hall in Leicestershire in 1806. Reading aloud, like truly engaged conversation, is badly in need of revival. I recently read "Tintern Abbey" aloud to my first-year course. In the discussion afterwards, one student picked up the line "For thou art with me here upon the banks/ Of this fair river . . ." and asked whether Wordsworth was quoting Psalm 23: "For thou art with me, thy rod and thy staff comfort me." I replied that Wordsworth is very likely doing so, especially as an earlier verse of the Psalm goes: "He shall feed me in a green pasture: and lead me forth beside the waters of comfort." Wordsworth and Dorothy are walking in a "green pastoral landscape" beside the River Wye. In my experience, students are more likely to pick up such echoes, allusions, and textures when they listen as well as read. Marshall McLuhan describes the difference cogently. In oral interchange, ". . . there are numerous simultaneous vistas of any topic whatever. The subject is looked at swiftly from many angles; classic notions and insights concerning that subject are, via memory, on the tip of every tongue in the intimate group." (Hawkes 52)

In processing the written word, however,

". . . the reader's eye not only prefers one sound, one tone, in isolation; it prefers one meaning at a time. Simultaneities like puns and ambiguities—the life of spoken discourse—become, in writing affronts to taste, floutings of efficiency." (Hawkes 52)

Lorca, writing about the peculiarly Spanish concept of *duende*, that gut feeling of authenticity, which "squeezes lemons of daybreak", is close to McLuhan's "simultaneous vistas":

"All the Arts are capable of possessing *duende*, but naturally the field is widest in music, in dance, and in spoken poetry, because they require a living body as interpreter—they are forms that arise and die ceaselessly, and are defined by an exact present." (Gili 132-3)

This tip-of-the-tongueness in an exact present is a timeless moment, what Blake called the "Moment in each Day that Satan cannot find." (Johnson and Grant 295). Of course, in art of any worth, there is an intellectual cement, a fluid architecture. But one is inclined to agree with Terence Hawkes when he observes that writing, far from being a reproduction, is more a reduction, of living speech (51). The Romantics struggled with this enigma: that to commit a thought to paper is to "sentence" it to a kind of death. Shelley, in morbid but brilliant mood, sums up this aspect of writing: ". . . this jingling food for the hunger of oblivion, called verse." (McFarland 168). That so much of the work of the Romantics has cheated oblivion and lives in our memories is testimony to their arduous struggle with this demon. One is tempted to exclaim with Dante in the *Purgatorio*: "And here let poetry rise again from the dead." (Canto 1. 8). That would be a *dolce stil nuova* indeed.

Another neglected aspect of oral culture is the premium it puts on a ready memory—the story-teller or reciter can call on an extensive repertoire of paradigms and plots and narrative tricks, enabling a change of direction, if desired. From what we know of the composition of "Tintern Abbey", it was carried in the poet's head for days, and written down when the walkers reached Bristol. One can imagine, on the one hand, relief in consigning it to paper; on the other, reluctance to lose the immediacy of the fructifying moments near the abbey itself. This Mozartian process of composition probably felt like moving from "wild ecstasies" to "sober pleasures." In several classes recently, I have set assignments where, instead of a written task, students can opt to learn a poem by heart, recite it to the class, and comment on it orally. Those who chose this option were pleasantly surprised at how relatively superficial most silent readings are. They were intrigued and thrilled by the process of reading, marking, learning, and inwardly digesting that this choice necessitated. Furthermore, the rest of the class were charmed and surprised at how differently the poems sounded, coming as they did from the body of the learner, not just the head. In this way, students can build up a "body of knowledge" as opposed to a bunch of facts. And it certainly helps if the teacher enjoys weaving spontaneous quotations and allusions and echoes into the warp and weft of the content-driven discourse.

To come to the third segment of my argument: the return to the sensuous. Thomas McFarland, in his book *Romanti-*

cism and the Heritage of Rousseau, uses throughout the book the metaphor of touching the weave of the great tapestry of Romanticism (I allude to this in my first paragraph). The ramifications of the word "touch" are relevant to my theme as well. For example, when someone has lost perspective, we say that he or she is "out of touch"; when we want to continue in communication with someone, we say: "keep in touch"; when performers are below par, we talk of them "losing their touch"; a musical toccata "was originally a piece intended to show touch technique, and the word comes from the feminine past participle of *toccare*, to touch" (Ackerman 71); when we are moved by a generous gesture, we say we are "touched"; it is no coincidence that mentally disturbed people are sometimes described as "touched"; we talk of "the touch of the poet", of the "common touch", of the "natural touch", and of over-emotional people as "touchy" (Rousseau was a typical example). I have already quoted Pope's lines on the "spider's touch"; when reading those lines, we can picture the filigree of a spider's web, that natural and fragile mandala. In the mandala of Romanticism, an adjustment to any one part sends a quiver throughout the whole design. Teachers of Romanticism should become like Whitman's "Noiseless, Patient Spider" launching forth "filament, filament, filament . . ." "Till the gossamer thread you fling catch somewhere, O my soul." Finding and imparting this true sense of touch keeps us what Whitman in another poem calls "Aplomb in the midst of irrational things" (Hall 158, 132).

In *The Spell of the Sensuous: Perception and Language in a More-Than-Human World*, the philosopher and ecologist David Abram presents a powerful argument for coming to our senses. Although his emphasis is not literary, many of his paragraphs read like cogent analyses of the way Romantic authors process their awareness of nature, especially John Clare:

"Such hierarchies [intellectual assumptions that put human experience "above" nature] are wrecked by any phenomenology that takes seriously our immediate sensory experience. For our senses disclose to us a wild-flowering proliferation of entities and elements, in which humans are thoroughly immersed. While this diversity of sensuous forms certainly displays some sort of reckless order, we find ourselves in the midst of, rather than on top of, this order. We may cast our gaze downward to watch the field mice and the insects that creep along the bending grasses . . . yet, at the same moment, hawks soaring on great winds gaze down upon our endeavors. Melodious feathered beings flit like phantoms among the high branches of the trees, while other animate powers, known only by their traces, move within the hidden depths of the forest . . . Does the human intellect, or "reason," really spring us free from our inheritance in the depths of this wild proliferation of forms? *Or on the contrary, is the human intellect rooted in, and secretly borne by, our forgotten contact with the multiple nonhuman shapes that surround us?*" [Abram's emphases]. (48)

That passage also reads like an elaboration of Keats's doctrine of Negative Capability, as exemplified in passages such as the following from his letters: ". . . if a sparrow come before my window I take part in its existence and pick about the gravel"; "I lay awake last night—listening to the Rain with a sense of being drown'd and rotted like a grain of wheat"; ". . . let us open our leaves like a flower and be passive and receptive." (Gittings 38, 89, 66).

And in an article lamenting the Enlightenment neglect of

"the rights of nature," Jonathan Bate makes a point similar to Abram's:

"Postmodernity proclaims that all marks are textmarks, but I believe we must hold fast to the possibility that certain textmarks called poems can bring back to our memory humankind's ancient knowledge that without landmarks we are lost." (Rights 6)

In the shortest and most haunting of the "Lucy" poems, Wordsworth uses the word "touch" with exquisite aptness, first, to imply immunity from change and suffering, second, to rub in the radical change in the second verse when Lucy is like one of nature's inanimate objects—out of touch indeed:

> A slumber did my spirit seal,
> I had no human fears;
> She seemed a thing that could not feel
> The touch of earthly years.
>
> No motion has she now, no force;
> She neither sees nor hears;
> Rolled round in earth's diurnal course
> With rocks and stones and trees.
> (Wu 327)

I once heard M. H. Abrams lecture for an hour on these lines. His respectful tracing of the web of meanings in this miniature masterpiece kept the listeners in touch with the mysteries of the poet's craft and art, and the lecture was a model for good teaching of Romanticism. In one of the best recent books about teaching, *The Courage to Teach: Exploring the Inner Landscape of a Teacher's Life*, Parker Palmer writes: "to teach is to create a space in which the community of truth is practiced." This community "is a complex and eternal dance of intimacy and distance, of speaking and listening, of knowing and not knowing." (90, 106). This "eternal dance of intimacy and distance" is a hallmark of Romanticism, and teachers and scholars in the field should cultivate it.

Touch is the foundation stone of Wordsworth's description in the Two-Part *Prelude* of his whole development, not just physical, but also mental and spiritual:

> From early days,
> Beginning not long after that first time
> In which, a babe, by intercourse of touch,
> I held mute dialogues with my mother's heart,
> I have endeavoured to display the means
> Whereby the infant sensibility,
> Great birthright of our being, was in me
> Augmented and sustained.
> (Wu 319)

The mature human being and artist is able to relate to the world because of that early "intercourse of touch":

> No outcast he, bewildered and depressed:
> Along his infant veins are interfused
> The gravitation and the filial bond
> Of nature that connect him with the world.
> (Wu 318)

A similar maternal and homely image is used by Dante at the climax of the Paradiso to convey the ineffability of the beatific vision:

Omai sara piu corta mia favella,
Pur a quell ch'io ricordo, che d'un fante
Che bagni ancor la lingua alla mammella.

["Now my speech will come more short even of what I remember than an infant's who yet bathes his tongue at the breast."] (Sinclair 482)

This swoop from the sublime to the meticulous detail is a function of that "grand elementary principle of pleasure" that Wordsworth celebrates in the Preface to *Lyrical Ballads* (Wu 361). Another heir of authentic Romantic sensuousness—Gerard Manley Hopkins—who could not be accused of wallowing in the sensual, wrote a sonnet "To R. B." [Robert Bridges], whose first line exalts "The fine delight that fathers thought . . ." (Gardner 68). Delight is the "gravitation and the filial bond" that bathes the infant's and the poet's tongue.

Jonathan Bate reminds us that the word "environment" did not appear until 1830, at a time when the two meanings implicit in the word "culture" were beginning their irrevocable divorce—the cultivation of the earth and the cultivation of our minds (Song 3-8). Contemporary teachers and scholars in the "field" of Romanticism are attempting to effect a reconciliation between these "two cultures"—and it is from the great Romantics that we can learn the art of this humane husbandry.

In the Romantic quest for inter-relationships, symbolic utterance plays a key role. The nature of reality as these writers saw it cannot be reduced to a set of rules or formulae; the swerve from minute particular to the vast unknown is the province of symbol. Hans-Georg Gadamer, in "The Relevance of the Beautiful," explains the function of the symbol:

"What does the word "symbol" mean? Originally it was a technical term in Greek for a token of remembrance. The host presented his guest with the so-called *tessera hospitalis* by breaking some object in two. He kept one half for himself and gave the other half to his guest. If in thirty or fifty years' time, a descendant of the guest should ever enter his house, the two pieces could be fitted together again to form a whole in an act of recognition.

". . . for our experience of the symbolic in general, the particular represents itself as a fragment of being that promises to complete and make whole whatever corresponds to it. Or, indeed, the symbol is that other fragment of being that has always been sought in order to complete and make whole our own fragmentary life. . . . the experience of the beautiful, and particularly the beautiful in art, is the invocation of a potentially whole and holy order of things, wherever it may be found." (31-2)

The nature of Romantic experience is fragmentary, but, paradoxically, that is what gives it meaning, because the fragment is always engaged in the desire and pursuit of the whole. This should be good news to today's students, who feel overwhelmed with "information overload" and often find difficulty making connections between their often impressive areas of knowledge. William James in *Principles of Psychology* (1890) uses a vivid image of the reductionist mentality, which claims "a river consists of nothing but pailsful, spoonsful, quartpotsful, barrelsful" of water. Romantic symbolism, as McFarland points out, is close to the authentic image as defined by James:

"Every definite image in the mind is steeped and dyed in the free water that flows round it. With it goes the sense of its relations, near and remote, the dying echo of whence it came to us, the dawning sense of whither it is to lead. The significance, the value, of the image is all in this halo or penumbra that surrounds and escorts it." (McFarland 298)

This "dawning sense of whither it is to lead" is close to Wordsworth's "something evermore about to be" in the Crossing the Alps section of the *Thirteen-Book Prelude*:

> Our destiny, our nature, and our home,
> Is with infinitude, and only there—
> With hope it is, hope that can never die,
> Effort, and expectation, and desire,
> And something evermore about to be.
> (Wu 391)

Skilful teaching of Romanticism should always nourish this "dawning sense" of an active imagination. For example, the Romantics, especially Wordsworth and Coleridge, were fascinated by rivers. Rivers, streams, waterfalls, springs, and fountains constantly irrigate the landscape of their work. Their awareness of moving water in all its manifestations, both philosophical and sensuous, has come to permeate our awareness of their own work as fluid, meandering, circular, powerful, and at times destructive. In short, since the Romantics, we cannot step into the same poem twice.

McFarland quotes a passage from Goethe (1797) distinguishing allegory and symbol, which will bring us full circle to our theme of indirections:

"Today there are also works of art that sparkle by virtue of reason, wit, gallantry and we include in this category all allegorical works as well; of these latter we expect the least, because they likewise destroy our interest in representation itself, and shove the spirit back upon itself, so to speak, and remove from its field of vision all that is truly represented. The allegorical differs from the symbolic in that what the symbolic designates indirectly, the allegorical designates directly." (299)

We all know those superficially sparkling works, often couched in jargon, which "shove the spirit back upon itself" and "remove from its field of vision all that is truly represented." Or, to revert to my homely metaphor, works that empty the baby with the bath water. Students today want to be in touch with the world and themselves, they want to be touched by works of art; they admire the common touch, but need to be shown the difference between the sublime simplicity of true works of art and what Wordsworth in the Preface to *Lyrical Ballads* calls "gross and violent stimulants" (Wu 359) that so often pass for profundity. While touching the weave of the fabric, they also want to feel connected to those invisible looms whose shuttles are forever stitching and unstitching our lives.

One of my earliest pupils, the Irish sculptor, Michael Warren, recently gave a lecture in Galway culminating in his artistic credo. While Warren works in an idiom ostensibly far removed from the Romantic, nothing could better demonstrate the fundamental retouching and cleansing of the doors of our perceptions effected by Romanticism in every corner of modern art:

"It is precisely when a creative intelligence at its most attentive is directed at matter here and now, in all its density and intractability, and an attempt is made to express what is always inexpressible, to hear what is always silent, that the object is transcended and a reality beyond the immediate is touched."

ONLINE RESOURCES

"Elementary Teaching" by Northrop Frye: http://www.mrbauld. com/fryepoet.html

Michael Warren's website is: www.michaelwarren.ie; see also retrospective catalogue listed in PRINTED SOURCES under Peter Murray.

PRINTED SOURCES AND FURTHER READING

Abram, David. *The Spell of the Sensuous: Perception and Language in a More-Than-Human World.* New York: Pantheon Books, 1996.

Ackerman, Diane. *A Natural History of the Senses.* New York: Random House, 1990.

Bate, Jonathan. *The Song of the Earth.* Cambridge, Mass.: Harvard University Press, 2000.
_____. *Romantic Ecology.* London: Routledge, 1991.

_____,ed. *"I AM": The Selected Poetry of John Clare.* New York: Farrar, Straus and Giroux, 2003.

_____ "The Rights of Nature." John Clare Society Journal, 14 (July 1995), 7-15.

Brownlow, Timothy. *John Clare and Picturesque Landscape.* Oxford: Clarendon Press, 1983.

Butt, John, ed. *The Poems of Alexander Pope.* London: Methuen, 1965.

Cobb, Edith. *The Ecology of Imagination in Childhood.* New York: Columbia University Press, 1977.

Foster, J. W. ed. *Nature in Ireland.* Dublin: Lilliput Press, 1997.

Gadamer, Hans-Georg. *The Relevance of the Beautiful and Other Essays.* Cambridge: Cambridge University Press, 1986.

Gardner, W.H., ed. *Gerard Manley Hopkins.* Harmondsworth: Penguin, 1963.

Gili, J. L., ed. *Lorca.* Harmondsworth: Penguin, 1967.

Gittings, Robert, ed. *Letters of John Keats.* London: Oxford University Press, 1970.

Hall, Donald. *A Choice of Whitman's Verse.* London: Faber and Faber, 1968.

Hawkes, Terence. *Metaphor.* London: Methuen, 1972.

Hayden, John O. ed. *William Wordsworth: The Poems.* Harmondsworth: Penguin, 1977.

Hudson, Roger. *Coleridge among the Lakes and Mountains.* London: Folio Society, 1991.

Johnson, Mary Lynn and John E. Grant, eds. *Blake's Poetry and Designs.* New York: W. W. Norton, 1979.
Kirkpatrick, Betty, ed. *Brewer's Concise Dictionary of Phrase & Fable.* Oxford: Helicon, 1992.

McFarland, Thomas. *Romanticism and the Heritage of Rousseau.* Oxford: Clarendon Press, 1995.

McKusick, James. "The Ecological Vision of John Clare." University of Toronto Quarterly, Winter 1991-2.

144

Murray, Peter. *Michael Warren: Light, Gravity and Distance.* Cork: Crawford Municipal Art Gallery, 2002.

Nettle, Daniel and Suzanne Romaine. *Vanishing Voices: The Extinction of the World's Languages.* Oxford: Oxford University Press, 2000,

Ong, Walter J. *Orality and Literacy.* London: Routledge, 1982.

Palmer, Parker. *The Courage to Teach: Exploring the Inner Landscape of a Teacher's Life.* San Francisco: Jossey-Bass, 1998.

Perkins, David. "How the Romantics Recited Poetry." Studies in English Literature 31 (1991): 655-671.

Sinclair, John D. *Dante's Paradiso.* New York: Oxford University Press, 1961.

Stubbs, Marcia and Sylvan Barnet. *The Little, Brown Reader.* Boston: Little, Brown,1977.

Worthen, John. *The Gang.* New Haven, Conn.: Yale University Press, 2001.

Wu, Duncan. *Romanticism: An Anthology.* Oxford: Blackwell, 1999.

Zinsser, William. *Writing to Learn.* New York: Harper & Row, 1988.

12

THE SINGING-MASTERS OF MY SOUL

In his biography of Laurence Olivier, *Olivier*, Anthony Holden describes how the great actor had an almost super-stitious reluctance to embark on a performance of *Othello*. Before he finally undertook what he called the "monstrous burden" of this part (in a legendary production of the early sixties), this seasoned actor went on a six-month voice-train-ing course. From the very first read-through of the script, usually a relaxed affair, the other actors were "pole-axed" by Olivier's reading, their blood running cold when, in Act 3, Iago's poison begins to take effect: "And O, you mortal en-gines whose rude throats/ Th'immortal Jove's dread clamours counterfeit,/ Farewell! Othello's occupation's gone." Nor-mally speaking in the tenor range, Olivier had succeeded in lowering his voice by a whole octave. (460-8)

This story should remain in our minds as a model of humble mastery—acting, among other things, involves the speak-ing of language, often, as in Shakespeare's case, heightened language, dramatic poetry. What we do at a typical reading of our own work is usually less demanding than taking on a dramatic role, but I maintain it is still impersonating a role, and it is (or should be) a dramatic situation. In other words, reading aloud, even one's own humble work, is an art, with all the connotations that word implies: awareness of an audience; pitch of voice; tone of voice; variations of tempo; attention to pauses; sense of occasion. All this, like any art, takes endless practice, and sometimes results in that triumph of communication where a speaker/actor/musician creates a temporary community of listeners. I once heard a literary critic (this was obviously before the 1980s) compare the skilful recitation of poetry to the art of singing opera, and I think the analogy is still apt.

In Ireland, you can pick eloquence out of the air waves—a kind of spiritual radio station. How else has such a small country won four Nobel Prizes for literature in the past eighty years? And that's not counting the most obsessed word-bibber of them all: Joyce. Everyday speech in Ireland still has a Shakespearean richness and rhythmical diversity. The Irish may have largely jettisoned their native tongue, but they beat the English at their own game. J. M. Synge tells us in the Preface to *The Playboy of the Western World* (1907) that he "got more aid than any learning could have given [him], from a chink in the floor of the old Wicklow house where [he] was staying, that let [him] hear what was being said by the servant girls in the kitchen." (Saddlemyer 96). Eavesdropping, yes, but Synge was an eavesdropper of genius, not interested in gossip but in rhythm. Far from writing what his detractors call Synge-song, he created a new dramatic music: plangent, extravagant, and inimitable.

Synge is an exemplary artist in that he brought the sophistication of his background and education to bear upon quite different material. One characteristic of great periods of artistic achievement is the ease with which "high" culture is blended with "pop" culture. Shakespeare moves seam-

147

lessly from court to tavern to battle scene. Unfortunately, this desirable marriage is usually short-lived in any cultural movement; the norm seems to be, as in contemporary society, an irrevocable divorce between the two worlds. One of the excitements of the sixties was a feeling that this consummation was possible. This process had started, in my experience, in the late fifties, that much maligned decade. Take 1956: Louis Armstrong toured Europe as Ambassador Satch: the extraordinary energy of his All Stars, whom I heard live, still rings in my ears. Lerner and Loewe launched their musical, *My Fair Lady*, still after fifty years a huge commercial success, and, in its way, worthy of its original: Shaw's *Pygmalion*. Elvis the Pelvis burst to fame about 1957, knocking the crooning Bing Crosby off his pedestal. Elvis may not appear a candidate for high culture, but the present dowager Duchess of Devonshire, one of the Mitfords, is a lifetime devotee. A few years later, at student parties, an entirely new electric and electrifying sound rang out— "Hey Jude" by the Beatles. By the spring of 1964, the sixties had definitely arrived. And then there was Bob Dylan, Donovan, and my favourites: Simon and Garfunkel. In a recent book—*Break, Blow, Burn*—Camille Paglia discusses Joni Mitchell's "Woodstock" in the company of great poems (225-32). What happened to this mood? Yuppies happened. The true leaders of the sixties, in every field, were all about a Blakean expansion of consciousness. The yuppies were all about expansion of bank balances.

The sixties were not just productive of great popular music; poetry readings flourished, as probably never before or since. Behind the then Iron Curtain, Yevtuschenko filled stadiums giving readings to word-hungry Russians; Spoken Arts long-playing records sold consistently—my first real exposure to Robert Frost, T. S. Eliot, Yeats, and the famously booming Dylan Thomas were at little gatherings around the gramophone in student rooms. Many lecturers were superb readers: imprinted on my mind are the sounds of poems by Donne, Hardy, and Hopkins recited by Alec Reid at Trinity, and the young poet and don Brendan Kennelly, who went on to edit *The Penguin Book of Irish Verse,* used to stop me in Front Square to recite a poem in progress. I went for ten-mile walks in the Dublin and Wicklow mountains, my eloquent companion, the journalist and broadcaster Ulick O'Connor, keeping up a constant stream of quotations. I used to meet Eavan Boland, then about twenty, for three-hour sessions in Dublin cafés, attracting stares as the surrounding patrons overheard her chanting, and enchanting, recitations. As young editors, Rivers Carew and I on *The Dublin Magazine* invited the young Seamus Heaney, one book already under his belt, to read in a Dublin theatre—this was a new and impressive noise in Irish, subsequently world, poetry. I met the French poet, Jacques Prévert, in Paris; I had studied his poems at school, and knew by heart his short pieces as masterfully sung by Yves Montand. The Italian poet Quasimodo read in Dublin in beautiful Italian; the Irish short story writer, Frank O'Connor, recited Yeats's "One that is ever kind said yesterday . . ." in Trinity, the greatest recitation I have ever heard. The Dublin theatres were crammed with articulate actors, Cyril Cusack bringing a Moscow Arts Theatre production of *The Cherry Orchard* to the Abbey Theatre, a soul-wrenching performance. And over the Irish Sea at the newly founded Royal Shakespeare Company at Stratford-Upon-Avon, the great director John Barton was revolutionising the speaking of Shakespeare's verse, having at his fortunate disposal the young voices of Ian McKellan, Ben Kingsley, Patrick Stewart, Anthony Hopkins, and the seasoned Dame Sybil Thorndike.

After several decades of yuppie sneering and posturing, in which jargon has erected its own iron curtain of obscurity, in which theory has been exalted over creative work, it is putting it mildly to say that the spoken arts are now much in need of a revival. The causes for the decline in good speaking are many and complex, and yuppies and television are not the only culprits. There is the strange belief that speaking well is élitist; there is the massive emphasis in most education on silent, analytical reading (in the ancient world, silent reading was itself suspect—Saint Ambrose once came across a solitary monk reading a psalter and asked him, "Why are you not reading aloud?") Most insidious of all, there is the, to me, wrong-headed view espoused by many academics since about 1980, that the sound of literature is unimportant; intellectual depth and political relevance is everything. But let me ask these hard-boiled eggheads: was there ever a writer worth his or her salt who was oblivious to verbal music?

Verbal music. Yes, you can have too much of a good thing. The modernist reaction against late Victorian literature, epitomised by T. S. Eliot, was partly a revolt against the musical excesses of writers such as Swinburne, William Morris, and Tennyson on an off-day. (Tennyson on a good day is a master of verbal harmony: "The moan of doves in immemorial elms/And murmuring of innumerable bees" is pretty good stuff, and not just pretty. My obvious relish in its sumptuous evocation of a summer's day would earn me sneers in many English departments.) Detractors of that gifted generalist, William Morris, like to think of him as weaving fabrics with one hand, while churning out endless mellifluous but vacuous verses with the other. Well, you can't do it all; anyone who designs wallpaper like Morris can be forgiven for overproduction as a poet. Yeats, who was a master of concentrated verbal music, once described Shaw's prose style as that of a sewing machine, endlessly clicking away. Such are the profound insights of rivalry. So, you can overdo the musicality of language. As Mallarmé was fond of saying, poetry is made of words.

If modern critics have turned their back on music, they often treat a poem as a visual artefact. Yes, you can see the shape of poems on the page, and some concrete poetry is very effective. But words are notoriously intangible, in English at any rate. I envy writers and readers of Chinese, who still see pictures in their letters. A poem, however, is not an artefact like a porcelain bowl or a sculpture. Can you tap it to see if it is hollow? Can you kick it, as Dr. Johnson once kicked a stone to refute what he regarded as an unacceptable idealism of Berkeley's? No, it is immaterial.

This brings us back to verbal music. Another characteristic poetry shares with music is the fact that a poem exists in time as well as having a partial spatial existence. Dante's *Divine Comedy* may be an artefact as a three-volume book, but a full experience of the poem can only be obtained by living with the work over time, preferably a lifetime. And although you can see the shape of a short poem on the page, the vibrations of the rhythms in the inner ear and how these echo and interlace over time is much more fascinating. Listening has become such an unpractised art that this kind of sophistication is now rare. But it was taken for granted by past generations, and is still a hallmark of outstanding talent. Listen to a contemporary master explain the subtleties of a modernist master. This is the opening paragraph of Seamus Heaney's essay "Englands of the Mind":

"One of the most precise and suggestive of T. S. Eliot's critical formulations was his notion of what he called 'the auditory imagination', 'the feeling for syllable and rhythm, penetrating far below the conscious levels of thought and feeling, invigorating every word; sinking to the most primitive and forgotten, returning to the origin and bringing something back', fusing 'the most ancient and the most civilised mentality.' I presume Eliot was thinking here about the cultural depth-charges latent in certain words and rhythms, that binding secret between words in poetry that delights not just the ear but the whole backward and abysm of mind and body; thinking of the energies beating in and between words that the poet brings into half-deliberate play; thinking of the relationship between the word as pure *vocable*, as articulate noise, and the word as etymological occurrence, as symptom of human history, memory and attachments." (*Finders Keepers* 81)

Neither Eliot nor Heaney wants to separate intellectual energies, human history, and articulate noise: these all earn compound interest, in both senses, by being consolidated in the same poetic bank account. And it is typical of Heaney's superbly well-stocked mental bank account that he deftly weaves a phrase by Shakespeare into his own writing. In Act One of *The Tempest*, Prospero asks Miranda: "What seest thou else/ In the dark backward and abysm of time?/ If thou remembrest aught ere thou cam'st here,/ How thou cam'st here thou mayst." (I,ii,49-52) Like a modern psychoanalyst, the world-weary Prospero is asking his innocent daughter Miranda to look into the scary but wonderful universe of buried memory for hidden secrets. This is what a good reader does. It is as if the mind activates a search key, encouraging the brain to scan the vast reservoir of one's past reading, much of it forgotten at a conscious level, and to match present ideas with long-past images and rhythms. I believe that one characteristic of writers of genius is this ability to access past sensation. A famous example, even quoted in books of psychology, is the "madeleine" passage in Proust's *In Search of Lost Time*. The adult narrator, Marcel, is given scented tea into which the custom is to dip a sponge cake or biscuit called a *madeleine*, a treat he remembers having had in childhood. The aroma propels Marcel into an extended recreation of childhood sensation, with every circumstantial detail intact.

Another example of the workings of this supra-rational process is the way that good writing often replicates, in its very rhythms, what it is describing. At the age of twenty-one, Coleridge wrote a world-weary sonnet to his childhood river, "To the River Otter." He remembers an activity known to so many children, that of skimming a flat stone over the surface of calm water. The memory is vividly enhanced by the perfectly apt rhythms:

> What blissful and what anguished hours, since last
> I skimmed the smooth thin stone along thy breast,
> Numbering its light leaps!
> (Wu 598-9)

"Numbering its light leaps." I defy you to read this, aloud or silently, without playing a brief movie in your mind of that bouncing stone.

One would give a lot to have tape recordings of the Romantic poets reading. David Perkins in his article "How the Romantics Recited Poetry" gives us some intriguing clues: Shelley was described as having an unpleasantly shrill voice, but we know something of Coleridge's and Wordsworth's delivery from some marvellously evocative descriptions. Hazlitt writes that Coleridge "read aloud with a sonorous and musical voice," instilling in the listener a "sense of a new style and a new spirit in poetry . . . It had to me something of the effect that arises from the turning up of the fresh soil, or of the first welcome breath of spring." (Wu 780). Hazlitt describes Wordsworth's "deep guttural intonation, [with] a strong tincture of the northern *burr*, like the crust on wine." (Wu 780). And the artist Haydon remembers Wordsworth "repeating Milton with an intonation like the funeral bell of St Paul's and the music of Handel mingled." (Wu 836). As far as scholars can infer from references such as these, the Romantics tended to chant when they read out loud. Jane Austen, their more level-headed contemporary, must have heard a lot of chanting in that she chooses to satirise the Romantic Marianne in *Sense and Sensibility* by making her astonished that her more equable sister could fall in love with a man, Edward Ferrers, who reads the poems of Cowper so flatly when called upon to do his party piece. For the neo-classical Austen, it is a stroke against the dangerously seductive Willoughby that he reads aloud so beautifully. Lord Byron was not only, by all accounts, dangerously seductive in the flesh, but recited in a particularly marked chant that he had learned at his school, Harrow. The cult of sensibility also required a tear in the eye and a trembling tone during intense moments that we would find embarrassing today. Keats was a more straightforward reader, but there is no doubting his profound emotion at great passages. While George Felton Matthew described Keats's eye for poetry as "more critical than tender" (Perkins 665), Charles Cowden Clarke testifies that on hearing certain passages of Homer, Keats "sometimes shouted." (Gittings, *John Keats*, 130)

My title is taken, of course, from "Sailing to Byzantium" by Yeats. Yeats believed that "A poem is an elaboration of the rhythms of common speech and their association with profound feeling. To read a poem like prose . . . is to turn it into bad, florid prose." He admired William Morris's indignation after he heard a prosaic reading of one of his poems: "It cost me a lot of damned hard work to get that thing into verse." (*Essays and Introductions* 508). He claimed in "An Introduction for my Plays" that he had spent his life "clearing out of poetry every phrase written for the eye, and bringing all back to syntax that is for the ear alone." (*Essays and Introductions* 529). Like Mozart, Yeats had a remarkable and gifted father, who realised he had produced a genius, but who was himself not only an accomplished painter but a legendary talker, complicated sentences tumbling from his lips as naturally as other people would say "It's a nice day." In "Sailing to Byzantium," Yeats implies that, however good our education has been, it is up to us to create our own distinctive voice: "Nor is there singing school but studying/ Monuments of its own magnificence" (Finneran 193). We acquire our own voice by listening to the great writers—the singing-masters of our souls—and then emulating them. All writers should aspire to be like the fox-terrier in the famous His Master's Voice logo, cocking our ear to the huge phonograph of culture.

So, how do we want to read poetry? Do we want to sing, chant, intone, lilt, perorate, startle, shock, astonish, quietly impress with a considered reading, or, to heck, read it as the mood strikes? The spectrum goes all the way from Paul Valéry, the great French modernist poet, who wrote: "One should start from song, put oneself in the attitude of the singer, tune one's voice to the fullness of musical sound, and from that point descend to the slightly less vibrant state suitable to verse" (Perkins 666). The range of opinion continues through W. H. Auden, who wanted verse to sound like "the conversational speech of everyday" (Perkins 666). It hits rock bottom, in my opinion, in the following statement by David Wojohn, writing in 1985: "A poem can exist without it having to be performed . . . a poem . . . is an object that should be contemplated more than it should be declaimed . . . the performance of a poem, *in itself*, is not fundamentally artistic." (Perkins 666). My view is much nearer the top of that spectrum than the bottom, but so much comes into play: our personality, our voice, the nature of our writing, our cultural background. For example, Valéry's exalted pitch may well suit the French language, but it is a bit high-flown for English.

There is a saying about opera: "What is too silly to be said may be sung." How does opera make this irrational leap from silliness to sublimity? Well, listen to Placido Domingo sing Mozart, and the question is answered. Poetry needs the same treatment: the ridiculous, the profound, the eccentric, the strange elements of poetic art need the same leap into the universal, and I believe the human voice can do that. Perhaps that is why St Ambrose was so shocked by a silent reader—the spiritual element was lacking. In the beginning was the Word. And was there ever a more profound auditory imagination at work than when Wordsworth read the completed *Prelude* to Coleridge and others in January 1807? Coleridge wrote afterwards:

> Me, on whom
> Comfort from thee and utterance of thy love
> Came with such heights and depths of harmony,

Such sense of wings uplifting, that the storm
Scattered and whirled me, till my thoughts became
A bodily tumult!

Coleridge finishes: "And when I rose, I found myself in prayer!" (Wu 687-8)

I began this talk with a theatrical anecdote. Let me return to the theatre by reminding you of Hamlet's advice to the players who turn up at Elsinore. Again, although he is talking about how to act, he's mainly talking about how to speak in a dramatic situation:

" Speak the speech, I pray you, as I pronounced it to you—trippingly on the tongue; but if you mouth it, as many of your players do, I had as lief the town-crier had spoke my lines. Nor do not saw the air too much with your hand, thus, but use all gently . . . Be not too tame neither; but let discretion be your tutor. Suit the action to the word, the word to the action, with this special observance: that you o'erstep not the modesty of nature. For anything so over-done is from the purpose of playing, whose end, both at the first and now, was and is to hold as 'twere the mirror up to nature, to show virtue her own feature, scorn her own image, and the very age and body of the time his form and pressure." (*Hamlet*, 3,2,1-5,16-24)

The modesty of nature. One of my favourite Irish proverbs goes: "Listen to the sound of the river, and you will catch trout." Anglers will know at once what that implies. Writers and readers should take it to heart as well: poets are fishers of the souls of words as they quiver, dart, appear, and disappear in the resounding river of time.

13

ROUSSEAU: Taking the Rough with the Smooth

In the weeks leading up to the Storming of the Bastille, anyone strolling in the Place de la Bastille would have heard a
strange disembodied ranting coming from the direction of
the fortress itself. One of the eight inmates—of whom four
were lunatics—was the notorious Marquis de Sade, who had
been justifiably locked up for activities which earned him
his reputation; even by the standards of the eighteenth century, de Sade was a criminal outsider. His most lasting legacy
was in bequeathing his name to the language: the word sa-
dism—cruelty or the deliberate infliction of pain—is his dubious epitaph. This aristocratic outlaw lived in comparative
luxury in the Bastille, even having his private library transported there. He had ingeniously constructed a makeshift
megaphone from metal prison utensils, and evening after
evening, broadcast subversive messages from the ramparts.
The governor of the Bastille, nervous enough at the growing
hostility outside against this symbol of the old order, had de
Sade moved to another prison just a week before the mob
broke the prison's defences and liberated the remaining sev-
en inmates, who were rather disgruntled at being disturbed.
Thus had the ignoble noble turned demagogue.

But nobody was really paying attention, either to the rant from the ramparts or to the gist of de Sade's works. Kenneth Clark, in *Civilisation*, reminds us that de Sade saw through the cult of benign nature from the start: "Nature averse to crime? I tell you that nature lives and breathes by it, hungers at all her pores for bloodshed, yearns with all her heart for the furtherance of cruelty." (274). These words were written in 1792, and unfortunately, are much more applicable to events of the past two hundred years than Jean-Jacques Rousseau's belief that nature and human nature are benign and innocent. Of course, we want to believe Rousseau rather than de Sade, but wishful thinking is not a wise state of mind in which to grapple with perennial and intractable problems. My favourite definition of politics is "The art of the possible." The impassioned rhetoric of late eighteenth-century France, including Rousseau's, tended towards the idealistic, the bombastic, the unattainable—it was, in short, already what we call Romantic. Romanticism strives for the unattainable; it is part of its grandeur and tension. But it is a dangerous recipe for public affairs, which must start from where human beings really stand. In his magisterial book, *Citizens: A Chronicle of the French Revolution*, Simon Schama writes about the moral idealism of members of the Third Estate in the spring of 1789: "Many of them urged the abolition of the *petits spectacles*—the boulevard theatres—with a fervour that would have warmed the heart of Jean-Jacques Rousseau. As if following the apocalyptic rhetoric of Mercier, they wished to lance the poisoned carbuncle of city life and clean it of its mess. This was, of course, to ask for the impossible. But asking for the impossible is one good definition of a revolution." (322)

Possible and impossible; criminal and innocent; realistic and idealistic; nature and nurture: these paradoxes were central to the revolutionary era, and they still trouble us. In this debate, there is no doubt that Rousseau is an inescapable presence. One contemporary scholar, Thomas McFarland, calls Rousseau the most influential figure in the past two hundred and fifty years. This essay tries to assess something of this influence for good and for ill. There is hardly an area of human endeavour to which the various works of Rousseau cannot be applied: music; opera; botany; education; gardening; voyages of exploration; animal welfare; autobiography; the novel; gender relations; marriage; and political affairs is just a short list. I believe that Rousseau's influence is largely benign in cultural matters, but malign in political affairs, so this paper will be divided into Rousseauolitry and Rousseau-bashing. There is a lovely legend about Plato, that when he was an infant in his cradle, a swarm of bees settled on his lips, hence the mellifluousness of his style. Rousseau's style also casts a spell, so that the reader forgets, as with Plato, that bees can also sting. I want to argue that remarks—virtual slogans—such as "Man is born free and everywhere finds himself enslaved and in chains" may be culturally inspirational, but they contain dangerous half-truths that make conflict in the political realm inevitable. Verbal violence, such as Diderot's remark: "Man will not be free until the last monarch is strangled in the guts of the last priest" overtly invite violence and bloodshed. So begins the Romanticism of violence, which has continued to our own day, and is the dark legacy of Romantic idealism. But let us start with the benign Rousseau.

When Rousseau died in 1778, he was living on the estate

of his friend and patron, the Marquis de Girardin. Girardin had written a book on the English garden, and his park at Ermenonville, near Paris, was one of the first estates in France to adopt the principles of the English garden, which departed from the severe rigour of famous French gardens, such as Versailles and Vaux-le-Vicomte. The latter style dominated and regimented nature in an autocratic way, and thus was a visible embodiment of absolutism. The English garden moved away from this geometrical tyranny, and from the late seventeenth century on, started to allow nature to do its own thing, letting trees and climbers, for example, spill naturally over man-made structures. Addison, Shaftesbury, and Alexander Pope were pioneers in this process of liberating the limbs of trees, in creating artificial lakes that looked natural, in painting pictures with nature itself—a movement that culminated in the late eighteenth century in the fashion for the Picturesque. Needless to say, political parallels were made: English constitutional history had moved away from autocracy to what today would be called pluralism—a political structure capable of containing widely divergent beliefs and capable of evolutionary reform without violent innovation. Nature and nurture co-existed in visible harmony in the English garden, and they were often compared to actual Gardens of Eden. Rousseau's love of walking (a revolutionary and democratic act in itself at a time when you were either tilling the soil or travelling through the landscape in a coach), of solitude, of botanising, of ecstatic immersion in nature were all admired, especially in England. There is a famous painting by Joseph Wright of Derby of Sir Brooke Boothby, a landed proprietor who landscaped his property along Rousseauian principles, and who met the man himself when Rousseau came to England. In the painting, he is alone in a picturesque landscape, soiling his immaculate breeches by stretching down on the leafy ground, in his hand a copy of Rousseau's *First Dialogue*. (Hunt and Willis 33-46; 308-10)

Boothby was a member of a group of reforming Whigs in Lichfield, a thriving provincial city. John Brewer in *The Pleasures of the Imagination* describes the importance of such local figures as Thomas Day, a children's author; Erasmus Darwin, grandfather of Charles, himself an evolutionist and poet; and Richard Lovell Edgeworth, an Irish gentleman, inventor, educator, and father of Maria, later a famous novelist. There was also the celebrated Lichfield poet, Anna Seward (573-612). This liberal-minded group were enthusiastic readers of Rousseau; Thomas Day wrote: "Were all the books in the world to be destroyed, the second book I should wish to save, after the Bible, would be Rousseau's *Emile*. With a perspicuity more than mortal, Rousseau has been able at once to look through the human heart, and discover the secret sources and combinations of the passions." (598). Darwin published a scheme of female education; Day wrote one of the most successful children's books of the century; Boothby wrote a book of fables; and Edgeworth wrote instructional works for young children. As Brewer writes: "Their model of educational reform was Rousseau's *Emile*, which advocated practical instruction rather than book learning, play and encouragement rather than coercive punishment, and lots of fresh air and exercise, together with careful and considerate moral nurturing." (598)

Very Wordsworthian, we might say. In fact, much of early Wordsworth is versified Rousseau:

> Up, up my friend, and clear your looks!
> Why all this toil and trouble?

Up, up, my friend, and quit your books,
Or surely you'll grow double!

Books! 'tis a dull and endless strife;
Come hear the woodland linnet—
How sweet his music! On my life,
There's more of wisdom in it.

And hark, how blithe the throstle sings!
And he is no mean preacher;
Come forth into the light of things,
Let nature be your teacher.

One impulse from a vernal wood
May teach you more of man,
Of moral evil and of good
Than all the sages can.

Sweet is the lore which nature brings,
Our meddling intellect
Misshapes the beauteous forms of things—
We murder to dissect.

Enough of science and of art,
Close up those barren leaves;
Come forth, and bring with you a heart
That watches and receives.
(Wu 401-2)

Conservative critics never ceased to make fun of this kind of
thing, which becomes the great voice of English Romanticism. Francis Jeffrey opens a review of Wordsworth with the
pithy words: "This will never do," and goes on to describe
his writing as "a tissue of moral and devotional ravings in

which changes are rung upon a few very simple and familiar ideas." (Wu 714-20). But it was steeped in Rousseau, who had corresponded with the great Swedish botanist Linnaeus: "Alone with Nature and with you I spend happy hours walking in the countryside, and from your *Philosophia botanica* I get more real profit than from all other books on ethics." (Blunt 214). In other words, let nature, and Linnaeus, be your teachers. And when, during the entrancing initial year of Wordsworth's and Coleridge's friendship, Coleridge in "Frost at Midnight" addresses his baby son, invoking a natural education "in the light of things," we get pure Rousseau being converted into great poetry:

> Therefore all seasons shall be sweet to thee,
> Whether the summer clothe the general earth
> With greenness, or the redbreasts sit and sing
> Betwixt the tufts of snow on the bare branch
> Of mossy apple-tree, while all the thatch
> Smokes in the sun-thaw; whether the eave-drops fall
> Heard only in the trances of the blast,
> Or whether the secret ministry of cold
> Shall hang them up in silent icicles,
> Quietly shining to the quiet moon. (Wu 628)

When Rousseau visited England in 1766, he stayed with the philosopher David Hume. He also visited Lord Harcourt at Nuneham Courtenay, near Oxford, where there was a picturesque garden. Harcourt had been influenced by Rousseau's novel *La Nouvelle Héloise*, where the author had set his heroine in a paradisial garden free of all man-made structures, in itself a bold step, as the eighteenth-century garden was littered with temples, busts, grottoes, obelisks, and often follies such as mock ruins. There was an inscription at Nuneham from Rousseau himself: "*Si l'auteur de la nature est grand dans les grandes choses, il est très grand dans les petits.*" ("If the author of nature is impressive in big designs, he surpasses himself in creating little things.") A bust of Rousseau was added after his visit. At Ermenonville, Rousseau was buried on an island of poplars in the middle of the lake. Girardin had an inscription carved on the tomb, which became a place of pilgrimage: "*Ici repose l'homme de la nature et de la vérité.*" ("Here lies the man of nature and of truth.") (Hunt and Willis, 39-46; 308-310). Like Voltaire, Rousseau was not to rest in peace for long. Their remains were transferred to the Panthéon in Paris by the revolutionary government, where they continue their eternal dialogue. Preferring the cultural to the political Rousseau, I like to imagine him at rest in the idyllic heart of nature, with the soft rustling of poplar leaves and the lapping of little waves suiting the man who had responded to nature with all his senses, virtually changing the way we experience it.

While Rousseau was staying in England, he received a letter from Ireland, from Emily, Duchess of Leinster. In it the duchess offered Rousseau, "then holed up in Derbyshire in a state of advanced paranoia," an elegant retreat if he would educate her children. (Tillyard 245). Rousseau declined the offer. The duchess and her friends, like many eighteenth-century women, were great readers of novels; the publication of *La Nouvelle Héloise* was received with raptures and was a welcome change from the oppressive domestic scenes in Richardson and the breezy male style of Fielding. With its barely licit steamy love affair between Saint Preux and his beautiful pupil, Julie, the book was guaranteed to cause flutters in salon and boudoir. The book scandalised and seduced as it went. The duchess and her friends were also great admirers of the educational ideas in *Emile*; Emily's sister, married to Charles James Fox, the Whig statesman, writes in a letter to her: "Dear little Harry is a pleasant child to have here; he really works very hard all day out of doors, which is very wholesome and quite according to Monsr. Rousseau's system." (Tillyard 239)

There is a fascinating historical point to ponder here. One of Emily's sons was Lord Edward Fitzgerald, who was three years old at the time of Emily's request that Rousseau teach her children. Lord Edward, known in Ireland as Citizen Lord, went on to become involved in the United Irishmen, a reformist movement that turned revolutionary under the influence of the French Revolution. Edward, to his family's great grief, was executed by the British forces as a rebel after his part in the 1798 rebellion. A French fleet was turned back in Bantry Bay just before the rebellion. In Bantry House, a romantic estate overlooking the bay, there is an exhibition of memorabilia from that tense time. Thus, Lord Edward could have been taught as a boy by the man who, more than most other writers, had influenced the revolution that indirectly cost Edward his life.

Another aspect of the benign Rousseau is his love of animals. Sketches show him in solitary domestic bliss, surrounded by his cat and dog. In an age when overt callousness and indifference to animals was everywhere evident, such tenderness is very welcome. Descartes had claimed that animals are just biological machines, and therefore feel no pain. Rousseau's love of animals is of a piece with his love of plants and flowers, and it is allied to the new interest in indigenous peoples, children, and the disadvantaged. In all these areas, Rousseau's work is influential. His work is central in the mid- to late-eighteenth-century period known as the Age of Sensibility. English poets began to celebrate the animal kingdom, showing a marked tenderness towards it. Thomas Gray had a cat called Selena, and wrote "Ode on a Favourite Cat Drowned in a Tub of Goldfishes". Cowper identified with the "stricken deer" and wrote touching poems about Puss, Tiny, and Bess, his tame hares. "My cat Jeoffry," wrote Christopher Smart, "is an instrument for the children to learn benevolence upon . . . God be merciful to all dumb creatures in respect of pain." (KeithThomas 176). Even the gruff Doctor Johnson used to send his servant out to buy oysters for his cat, Hodge (Fleeman 1216). In his massively English down-to-earth way, Johnson rejects continental abstraction in favour of the companionship of animals: "I had rather see the portrait of a dog I know than all the allegories you can show me." (Pevsner 31). And, surprisingly, prisoners in the Bastille were allowed cats to keep down the vermin, but they must have provided companionship and amusement as well. This increased sensitivity to animals led to the foundation of the SPCA in 1824. There is an Irish expression I love, which seems to be obsolete elsewhere: "He's full of nature"—that is, full of affection and the milk of human kindness.

James Boswell, author of the great biography of his friend Doctor Johnson, had met Rousseau in France. Boswell, in his gushing way, is representative of the Age of Sensibility. Many incidents in the *Life of Johnson* are like a dialogue between the old and the new world, Boswell representing views that are close to Rousseau's, who was an oddity in eighteenth-century France in his loathing of Paris and the corruptions of the modern metropolis. Boswell once remarked to Johnson that even London had lost its zest for him. He was cut short by the famous retort: "Why, Sir, you find no man, at all intellectual, who is willing to leave London. No, Sir, when a man is tired of London, he is tired of life; for there is in London all that life can afford." (Fleeman 858-9). These sentiments would have been shared by Voltaire and Diderot, for whom Paris was where it was at, as we say. Rousseau retreating to Les Charmettes and Wordsworth living at Dove Cottage were regarded as almost deranged. They also walked everywhere and conversed with rustics. Crazy! To this day, there are denizens of New York, London, and Paris who rarely set foot in the countryside, and feel nothing lacking.

Rousseau was also musical, and had invented a new system of notation. His opera, *Le Devin du Village* (*The Village Soothsayer*), was regularly performed in Paris. Boswell told Johnson that music affected him to such a degree that he was ready to shed tears and to rush into the thickest part of the battle. Johnson's reply came with Anglo-Saxon bluntness: "Sir, I should never hear it, if it made me such a fool." (Fleeman 874). On another occasion, Boswell gave Johnson an account of his meeting with Captain Cook, and had "felt a strong inclination to go with him on his next voyage." Johnson's reply shows the limitations of his great classical learning: "Why, Sir, a man *does* feel so, till he considers how very little he can learn from such voyages." (Fleeman 722). On another occasion, Johnson claimed that a blade of grass was the same in one place as another. It was not something the rustic John Clare (a real local answer to Rousseau's "noble savage" dream) would have said just thirty years later. The French explorer Bougainville was a devotee of Rousseau, and when he got to Tahiti, thought he had indeed found the noble savage in a state of idyllic nature. Similarly, the hard-headed Yorkshireman, Cook, took a shine to a South Sea islander called Omai, and brought him to London where he was fêted by society, introduced to the King and painted by Joshua Reynolds.

As we can see, Rousseau crops up everywhere in late eighteenth-century culture. He was one of those figures who seems to epitomise what the Germans call the zeitgeist, the spirit of the age, which in itself was a new concept—the classicist believing all ages to be roughly similar, like blades of grass. Inevitably, this ferment of creation and enquiry led to the political realm, and, of course, Rousseau was in the thickest part of the battle there as well. The finer spirits of the time believed that a new age was dawning—*Novus Rerum Nascitur Ordo*—and this idealism is moving in retrospect. Wordsworth, looking back to the mood of 1790, remembers "France standing on the top of golden hours,/ And human nature seeming born again." (Jonathan Wordsworth et al. 204). By 1792, the Revolution had turned into anarchic cruelty and paranoiac tyranny; Wordsworth, who had hurriedly left France, leaving behind his lover and daughter, describes his anguish:

> Most melancholy at that time, O friend!
> Were my day-thoughts, my dreams were miserable;
> Through months, through years, long after the last beat
> Of those atrocities (I speak bare truth,
> As if to thee alone in private talk)
> I scarcely had one night of quiet sleep,
> Such ghastly visions had I of despair,
> And tyranny, and implements of death,
> And long orations which in dreams I pleaded
> Before unjust tribunals, with a voice
> Labouring, a brain confounded, and a sense
> Of treachery and desertion in the place
> The holiest that I knew of—my own soul.
> (Jonathan Wordsworth et al. 378)

What makes *The Prelude* such a great poem is the tension between Wordsworth's early illusioned view of the world and his brusquely disillusioned young adulthood. Everyone, just by growing up, has a similar progress, but Wordsworth's childhood and youth were unusually enchanted, his fall from grace extremely painful. It is a particularly emblematic modern journey: the "blessed mood" described in "Tintern Abbey" is suddenly confronted with the modern world at its most destructive. The shock drove Wordsworth to fall back on his inner resources, imagination eventually healing these familiar wounds. Wordsworth's detractors see this as political apostasy, but, like Edmund Burke, Wordsworth is being consistent. They were the first powerful minds to understand that tyranny can come as easily from the left as from the right. A sickening pendulum swing between left and right has been characteristic of the past two hundred years. Now, as then, it is imperative to find a third alternative, which balances opposing forces. Wordsworth found it in the Romantic imagination; Burke in the British Constitution. Pope, as so often, had put it with memorable succinctness in the "Epistle to Bathurst":

> "That secret rare, between th'extremes to move
> Of mad Good-nature, and of mean Self-love."
> (Butt 581)

The indefatigable Boswell tells of another exchange, which is extremely pertinent to this topic. During a political argument, Boswell turns to Johnson and says: "So, Sir, you laugh at schemes of political improvement." Johnson, as always, has an answer: "Why, Sir, most schemes of political improvement are very laughable things." (Fleeman 423). Now, before we write Johnson off as an unregenerate stick-in-the-mud, notice he says "most schemes" and remember that Englishmen of the eighteenth century had some justification for their dislike of theoretical innovation. Continental writers, such as Voltaire and Montesquieu, regarded England as a model worthy of emulation. Right back to Magna Charta in 1215, when the barons successfully confronted King John, through the English Reformation and the Elizabethan religious compromise, through the English Civil War, through the Glorious Revolution of 1688, which secured constitutional freedoms which were the envy of Europe, England had evolved a system of government that balanced what the French called the Three Estates: Nobility, Church, and People, or Lords of Church and State and Commons. This had not been achieved without turmoil—Henry VIII was no pussyfoot and the Puritans had already beheaded their King—but it was as stable as conditions of the time allowed and not something to throw away in the name of a theoretical perfectibility. Predictably, Johnson thought Rousseau "a very wicked man."

Burke described Rousseau with a milder adjective, but one showing more profound insight. For Burke, Rousseau is above all vain. I agree. For while part of me admires Rousseau's initiative in washing his dirty linen in public in *The Confessions,* I also believe that our modern obsession with deviant behaviour and the spectacularly insignificant private lives of celebrities can also be laid at his door. And, talking of laying things at doors, no decent person can forget or forgive Rousseau for 1) abandoning five of his children and 2) self-righteously trying to justify his decision. There are those who will argue that an artist's private life is of no consequence when considering his work. I disagree; I am unable to read Ezra Pound or listen to Wagner, because I find that their hysterically anti-democratic beliefs taint their work. Besides, Rousseau goes out of his way to parade his vices as well as his virtues, inviting the reader to regard them as indivisible. So callousness must be added to my indictment. Furthermore, everyone who writes about Rousseau admits that he suffered from unnecessary paranoia. Voltaire was also persecuted for his work; he fought back like a tiger in the name of justice, but he kept his humanity. Rousseau epitomises that modern phenomenon: callous self-righteousness acting in the name of theoretical virtue, and I believe it has been a pernicious influence in public affairs, from Robespierre on.

Rousseau's ideas became canonised by the early revolutionaries, especially by Robespierre, who, for a short period, became a self-appointed guardian of republican mores and executioner of all who disagreed with him. The mere possession of a book by Edmund Burke was enough for Robespierre to send the hapless reader to the guillotine. Either Rousseau's arguments are deeply flawed or open to dangerous misinterpretations. Admittedly, any historical thinker can be misconstrued and used selectively. But there is a strain of extremism in Rousseau—he thought, for example, that atheists should be put to death.

Rousseau's reaction against eighteenth-century reason, like Romanticism itself, sweeps us into dangerously indefinable depths. As he writes in *The Confessions*: "I felt before I thought: which is the common lot of man, though more pronounced in my case than in another's." (19). Burke, who was himself a romantic visionary, had predicted as early as 1790, when citizens in France were dancing round maypoles or planting liberty trees, that the revolutionaries would go on to kill their King and Queen, and that the celebration of abstract liberty would turn aggressive and conquering. He was, of course, correct. On the back of Goya's graphic masterpiece, "The Third of May 1808", in which a group of inconvenient Spanish peasants are being mown down by the rifles of a French revolutionary army firing squad, Goya wrote: "The sleep of Reason produces monsters." Goya's late paintings are full of monstrosities. As we know, the cruel indifference of nature is hard enough to bear—the mid-eighteenth century had been stopped in its optimistic tracks by the Lisbon earthquake—but man's inhumanity to man is much more disturbing and monstrous.

Rousseau is full of inconsistencies. Another of his puritanical extremisms is his opposition to the theatre. He disliked the smooth formalities of classical French theatre, finding it in cahoots with social and clerical power structures rather than being a valid criticism of society. Well, Racine's *Phèdre* is one of the great plays of the world, and Molière and Voltaire are no time-servers either. In his dislike of English culture, Rousseau obviously neglected to read Shakespeare deeply, especially the dark, tragic Shakespeare. The whole of *King Lear*, often described as the greatest post-classical play, is a deconstruction of Rousseau's world-view. Enter Edmond, the Bastard, whose view of nature is closer to de Sade than Rousseau:

> Thou, nature, art my goddess. To thy law
> My services are bound. Wherefore should I
> Stand in the plague of custom and permit
> The curiosity of nations to deprive me
> For that I am some twelve or fourteen moonshines
> Lag of a brother? Why "bastard"? Wherefore "base",
> When my dimensions are as well compact,
> My mind as generous, and my shape as true
> As honest madam's issue? Why brand they us
> With "base", "baseness, bastardy—base, base"—
> Who in the lusty stealth of nature take
> More composition and fierce quality
> Than doth within a dull, stale, tired bed

Go to th' creating a whole tribe of fops
Got 'tween a sleep and wake? Well then,
Legitimate Edgar, I must have your land.
Our father's love is to the bastard Edmond
As to th' legitimate. Fine word, "legitimate."
Well, my legitimate, if this letter speed
And my invention thrive, Edmond the base
Shall to th' legitimate. I grow, I prosper.
Now gods, stand up for bastards. (I, ii,1-22)

King Lear, almost unbearably, makes the spectator look into an abyss, the lusty stealth of nature and of human nature. It is Hobbes's nature: "poor, solitary, nasty, brutish, and short." Camille Paglia writes in *Sexual Personae*: "One cause of Rousseau's simplistic nature-theory: there was no *Faerie Queene* in French literature to show the dangers of nature. Consequently, Sade arose, with all his horrors, to check Rousseau's happy hopes. Rousseau and Sade together equal the totality of Spenser." (235). Adapting a phrase from Mozart's letters, I would say: "Melt Rousseau and Sade together and you wouldn't make a Shakespeare." Shakespeare's art goes through the underworld, and emerges in the sweetness of Cordelia, the exquisite language of the late plays, and what George Rylands called "the doctrine of forgiveness." But it is a tragic world—Cordelia and Desdemona die, along with many other innocents. Part of Shakespeare's point is that when human beings forget the limitations of their humanity, they become monstrous. As Troilus puts it in *Troilus and Cressida*: "This is the monstruosity in love, lady—that the will is infinite and the execution confined; that the desire is boundless, and the act a slave to limit." (Wells and Taylor, *Tragicomedies* 244). The dire consequence of unbridled and unprincipled human passions stalks through Shakespeare's imagination, especially in *King Lear*: "If that the heavens do not their visible spirits/Send quickly down to tame this vile offence,/It will come,/Humanity must perforce prey on itself/Like monsters of the deep." (Harrison 101)

Robespierre and the Jacobins ignored this Shakespearean insight. In the service of what Burke called "this conquering empire of light and reason," they were willing to murder large numbers of their contemporaries. In the early months of 1794, for example, scholars quoted by Schama have estimated that at least a quarter of a million people were murdered in the Vendée, a region in western France that wanted to keep traditional practices, such as the ministrations of their beloved priests, usually local boys. In Lyon, the "national razor" worked at a frantic pace, the record being proudly logged as twenty-five heads in thirty-five minutes. One revolutionary general in the Vendée suggested deporting the bulk of the region to Madagascar. Another general consulted a chemist to ascertain the possibility of using "gassings . . . to apyhxiate the enemy." Sound familiar?

This conquering empire of light and reason. How did Enlightenment progress become so perverted? Goya's painting "Saturn Devouring His Children" is an apt comment. Let me quote a few paragraphs by Michael Ignatieff from his life of Isaiah Berlin:

"Enlightenment rationalism supposed that conflicts between values were a heritage of mis-education or injustice and could be swept away by rational reforms, by indoctrinating individuals into believing that their individual interests could be fully realized by working exclusively for the common good. Both Rousseau and Robespierre envisaged just such a state, in which freedom was experienced as submission to rational necessity."

"Berlin evidently approved of the ideals of self-realisation. The danger lay in the idea, latent in Enlightenment rationalism and Romanticism alike, that men might be so blinded to their true natures—by ignorance, custom or injustice—that they could only be "freed" by those revolutionaries or social engineers who understood their objective needs better than they did themselves."

"'This is one of the most powerful and dangerous arguments in the entire history of human thought,' wrote Berlin. 'Let us trace its steps again. Objective good can only be discovered by the use of reason; to impose it on others is only to activate the dormant reason within them; to liberate people is to do just that for them which, were they rational, they would do for themselves, no matter what they in fact say they want; therefore some forms of the most violent coercion are tantamount to the most absolute freedom.'" (201-7)

Berlin's greatest contribution to liberal thought, I believe, is his distinction between negative and positive liberty. Negative liberty strives to free us from the familiar obstacles of tyranny, prejudice, or discrimination, leaving us to get on with life as we see fit. Positive liberty is aggressive and invasive: like Stalinism, it wants to bug our private spaces to listen for heresy; it wants to take over our very thoughts, and impose its own "mind-forged manacles." In his political thought, Rousseau is closer to the latter. He writes in *The Social Contract* that people may have to be (and the four telling words are his) "forced to be free." (Dunn 166). In other words, those who do not accept the whole package of the party line are outlaws; in times of duress ("*la patrie en danger*") they can be eliminated as so much rubbish on little or no evidence. Rousseau's concept of the General Will, from our position of dire retrospect, looks menacingly like twentieth-century dictatorships.

No doubt Rousseau, a gentle creature in his own life, would be amazed at the transmogrification of his ideas, if he were to revisit this distracted globe, this muddy vesture of decay. For me, the two fatal flaws in his work are vanity (like the Jacobins, he was convinced of his own virtue), and naiveté: given his lack of a tragic sense of life and his woozy trust that real virtue will always prevail, he opens the door to Edmond, Iago, Richard III, and Macbeth. Shakespeare's continuing mesmerising power is demonstrated by the fact that we don't need to think long before finding real-life figures who enact the diabolical deeds dreamed up by these fictional characters.

Berlin's other great contribution is his belief that, far from being indivisible, human character is tragically divided against itself. The pursuit of good may be laudable—we can all spout the catchwords of liberty, equality, and fraternity—but maybe we can't have all of these at once. Ignatieff writes about Berlin's insistence that "the self was torn by competing impulses; the ends and goals that human beings pursued were in conflict. Berlin made human dividedness, both inner and outer, the very rationale for a liberal polity. A free society was a good society because it accepted the conflict among human goods and maintained, through its democratic institutions, the forum in which this conflict could be managed peacefully." (203). For example, a liberal may have to defend the liberty of a minority against a democratic tyranny. Indeed, one could add, to be an intellectual or a writer in today's world is constantly to be called upon to do that.

5.

Rousseau was not alone in thinking that eighteenth-century society was full of corruption; it was a *leitmotif* of the century's writers. Where he differs from, say, Voltaire, is his apparent belief in past happiness and future perfectibility: nostalgia and utopianism. Both are dangerous ideas, based on no evidence whatsoever. The childhood of the human race, just as of each individual, is likely to have been one of dark fears, helpless dependence, and anarchic lusts and appetites. Rousseau did not appreciate Voltaire's famous quip that he had given up walking on all fours since infancy and he saw no reason to do so again. To claim that society is responsible for all our ills is an inflammatory half truth that invites resentment and violence. Voltaire, for all his courageous defence of individual liberties, would also have claimed that society is our only bulwark against the cruelty of nature and of human nature. It is again one of the themes of *King Lear*: "Allow not nature more than nature needs,/ Man's life is cheap as beast's." says Lear to Regan (Wells and Taylor, *Tragedies*, 291). And, confronted by Edgar disguised as a Bedlam beggar, Lear says:

"Thou wert better in a grave than to answer with thy uncovered body this extremity of the skies. Is man no more than this? Consider him well. Thou owest the worm no silk, the beast no hide, the sheep no wool, the cat no perfume. Ha, here's three on's are sophisticated; thou art the thing itself. Unaccommodated man is no more but such a poor, bare, forked animal as thou art." (Wells and Taylor, *Tragedies*, 300)

For Shakespeare, man in the natural state is relentlessly helpless and miserable; we owe everything to sophistication. As

Burke later wrote: "Art is man's nature." We need the accommodations of human society, inventiveness, and art to transcend our worm-like natures. The problem, of course, is compounded when human societies forget nature altogether, and sophistication becomes an end in itself. Keats, one of the most sensuous of poets, also knew what real suffering was; he writes in a letter: "But in truth I do not believe in this sort of perfectibility—the nature of the world will not admit of it—Let the fish philosophise the ice away from the Rivers in winter time." (Gittings, *Letters,* 249). Balance is all. But how do we achieve it? The following paragraph half way through Schama's book brilliantly explains what I am claiming is the wrong turning taken by the reforming zealots in the period following the storming of the Bastille, when the moderates attempted to install constitutional monarchy along British lines:

"At stake were not just picayune matters of institutional detail but a fault line that ran very deep in late eighteenth-century culture. Mounier and the "English" party were heirs to Montesquieu and, behind that, an Aristotelian tradition of seeing in diversity, divisions and balances a satisfying equilibrium. Their opponents, whether arguing from neoclassical rigour or from Rousseau-like consistency, were holists. For them, the *patrie* was indivisible, and they responded to charges that they were creating a new despotism of the many by retorting that the new, single sovereignty was a morally reborn animal that could have nothing in common with the impurities of the old. For Sièyes, whose debt to Rousseau's *Social Contract* was explicit, while the General Will was more than the sum of the wills that it comprised, it was, by definition, incapable of injuring the freedoms for which it was sovereign. Citizens were incapable, in this sense, of harming themselves." (444)

Well, we don't feel like morally reborn animals now. An unwholesome mixture of self-righteousness and naiveté, fuelled by paranoia, seems to have been transferred to the body politic from Rousseau's private life. In his justification for abandoning his five offspring to foundling homes, Rousseau assures us they will be better looked after than if they had remained in his, and his wife's, care. Poor Thérèse seems to have had no hearing from her husband in her desire to be a nourishing mother. Such callousness became a public habit: children were encouraged to stand up in tribunals denouncing their parents as traitors, a fact that especially shocked Burke, with his Irish love and reverence for family life.

In an essay written in 1943, when France was once again fighting for its life, the philosopher Simone Weil wrote "Draft for a Statement of Human Obligations." She divides our needs into those of the body and those of the soul. Bodily needs are straightforward: food, warmth, sleep, rest, exercise, fresh air. The needs of the soul are more complicated; she describes them in a series of complementary pairs "which balance and complete each other":

"The human soul has need of equality and of hierarchy."
"The human soul has need of consented obedience and of liberty."
"The human soul has need of truth and of freedom of expression."
"The human soul has need of some solitude and privacy and also of some social life."
"The human soul has need of both personal property and collective property."
"The human soul has need of punishment and of honour."

"The human soul has need of security and also of risk".

"The human soul has need of disciplined participation in a common task of public value, and it has need of personal initiative within this participation."

"The human soul needs above all to be rooted in several natural environments and to make contact with the universe through them." (Rees 219-27)

For me, the clarity and compassion of this essay, typical of her work, throws bridges across the void created by the fault line identified by Schama. It acknowledges the double-sided nature of Nature, and that seemingly contradictory standpoints can be part of the same conviction. Inner conflict, for the honest person, is the norm. A good society is one that allows individuals to work through these conflicts without creating real violence in the public domain.

We have seen that Rousseau is one of the most influential thinkers in modern history. The first part of my essay applauds him for his cultural and humanitarian influence; the second part takes him to task for having helped to launch the virus of theoretical innovation into the public realm. We are dealing with a complex, undoubtedly modern man, with a very mixed bag of tricks. He is one of the great stylists of the French language, and reading him is always stimulating. But I have held up other, to me, more powerful minds—Shakespeare, Burke, Isaiah Berlin, Simone Weil—who can help us find our way to some sense of balance in what Schama calls "the quotidian mess of the human condition." (875)

14

POETRY FOR SUPPER

"Listen, now, verse should be as natural
As the small tuber that feeds on muck
And grows slowly from obtuse soil
To the white flower of immortal beauty."

"Natural, hell! What was it Chaucer
Said once about the long toil
That goes like blood to the poem's making?
Leave it to nature and the verse sprawls,
Limp as bindweed, if it break at all
Life's iron crust. Man, you must sweat
And rhyme your guts taut, if you'd build
Your verse a ladder."

"You speak as though
No sunlight ever surprised the mind
Groping on its cloudy path."
"Sunlight's a thing that needs a window
Before it enters a dark room.
Windows don't happen."

So two old poets,
Hunched at their beer in the low haze
Of an inn parlour, while the talk ran
Noisily by them, glib with prose.
(*Selected Poems 1946-1968*, 53)

If music be the food of love, poetry is also an essential nutri-
ent in one's spiritual diet. Like music, poetry has contrasting
modes, from formal to informal utterance, from closed to
open form, from traditional to experimental styles: in classical terms, from the Apollonian to the Dionysian; in modern
terms, from the neo-classical to the romantic.

In this poem, "Poetry for Supper," R. S. Thomas deftly sets
up a dialogue between representatives of each side of this perennial see-saw in the arts. While the romantic speaker has
the first word, and the classicist the last word, so to speak,
neither is allowed to dominate or to claim the whole truth.
Poetry, it is implied, like food, grows out of a dark, prime-
val, chthonic soil before it aspires, like Blake's Sunflower,
toward "that sweet golden clime" of sunlight and beauty.
The sunflower may longingly lean in the direction of light,
but it is always rooted in the earth. Cultural history seems
to be an endless creation of forms along with an endless
dissolution of forms: once a paradigm is established, it is
altered, dismantled, and rebuilt before it becomes rigid and
static. In the *Poetics*, Aristotle describes every good plot as
a complication (an infolding), followed by a dénouement
(an unknotting, an unfolding). Great artists seem to enact
this larger historical process within their own evolution: the
serious artist will absorb existing formal conventions, will
be aware of a profound debt to all previous achievements in
the field, usually going on to dissolve them in the light of

individual experience, and to mint them anew in the chemical ferment of imagination. It could be called the Houdini syndrome: good artists positively relish being tested by formal demands, to be bounded in a nutshell; their task is then to untie knots, shatter the framework, in an audacious bid to become kings of infinite space. We can't be metaphysical until we're physical; even the most transcendent art has to get its feet soiled.

The classical artist has a Churchillian awareness of the sway and sweep of history, never forgetting the "long toil/That goes like blood to the poem's making", the need to "sweat/ And rhyme your guts taut"; the tears go with the territory. Beauty, as poets from Sappho through Baudelaire to Yeats have been aware, is a cold, distant, cruel, unattainable goddess, but that only sharpens their resolve never to surrender. A brief glimpse of "the white flower of immortal beauty" is sometimes vouchsafed after much ladder-building in the Yeatsian "foul rag-and-bone shop of the heart." (Finneran 348)

An awareness of the fragility of civilisation is also characteristic of the classical artist. Classicism stresses the need for constant vigilance of thought, for ritual cleansings to counteract the habitual tendency of human nature to sink into torpor, complacency, conformity, or worse. This ritualising of the aesthetic impulse is akin to the practices of the African tribe, the Elgonyi, described by Jung, who spit on their hands and hold them up to the sun at its rising. Jung explains they are not so much sun-worshippers as believers that the "*moment* in which light comes is God." (Jung 295-8). Each artist has a similar symbolic responsibility to civilisation: the poet, for example, should daily recite something akin to line 8 at the beginning of Dante's *Purgatorio*: "And here let poetry arise from the dead."

Those who aspire to be competent musicians are well aware of the step-by-step, arduous mastery of technical detail demanded: books of musical exercises, such as scales, are often called "*Gradus ad Parnassum*"—if you want to make the grade, surmount each rung of the ladder, you will need a dogged one-foot-in-front-of-the-other discipline. If you want to climb Parnassus, make sure you have the right equipment. The romantic often wants to short-circuit this process, believing intuition will soar where tuition plods, that inspiration will airlift them to the summit. The most influential figure in this Nature over Nurture stance is Rousseau, who can indeed soar on home-made wings, but who often gets tied in the knots of his own solipsism. What seems to have saved him from his own romancing was his dogged application to the principles of musical composition, which also brought him in a precarious living.

The Rousseauesque speaker of the first four lines, with a belief in an innate organic process, a faith in the creative possibilities of muck—a *nostalgie de la boue*—is countered by the classical obsession with past masters. The line from Chaucer referred to—"The lyf so short, the craft so long to lerne"—is the opening line of "The Parlement of Foules." (Robinson F. N. 310). Life is short, art is long, or it takes a lifetime to learn the rudiments of the craft or art. The romantic, now mysteriously elevated to a misty mountain path from the obtuse soil of the first verse, puts in a plea for surprise and spontaneity, that we can be surprised by joy. To which the classicist counters that sunlight is all very well, but to make a coherent work of art, it must be focused, channelled, by the concentrated lens of the mind. As a rule, windows don't happen, no matter how much we yearn for happenings.

Further evidence that the classicist stresses mental discipline and technical knowledge is hinted at in the phrase "dark room." This is a literal translation of the Italian phrase camera oscura—the name for an optical aid used by artists and designers that predated the camera. The phrase was adopted later for the place where photographic images were developed. Originally, the instrument ordered a view or landscape by reflecting it onto a slanted lens inside a box-like contraption, enabling an artist to sketch over the image on transparent paper. Artists equipped with such an instrument were aware that it was an analogue for the mind, that dark room with its ghostly unexplored corners. Some scholars believe that the uncanny verisimilitude of Vermeer's paintings, their spot-on roominess, was achieved by using these instruments. To the classicist, this is all in the day's work; to the romantic, there is a suspect reliance on instrumentality and malice of forethought. Great art, of course, transcends these divisions—the art gallery visitor, rapt in front of a picture such as *The Artist in his Studio*, couldn't give a hoot what technique was used to arrive at such a luminous destination. As for Chaucer, in his approximately sixty years of life, as well as being a diplomat and man of affairs, he also managed to put an indelible seal on the rapidly developing English language, inventing among other things the rhyming couplet, a form that had a brilliant showing up to Alexander Pope and beyond.

In the final verse, the two hunched poets with opposing views seem united in a *sotto voce* conspiracy against the noisy, glib, prosaic world around them. Poetry being their main sustenance, their tongues are loosened by liquor in the Falstaffian, Dionysian atmosphere of the inn parlour, with its low haze—a romantic underworld. This is not the front parlour kept traditionally sacrosanct, sheet-draped, dry-dusted, lace-curtained, and only used for rare occasions. This is Eastcheap, Night-town, Montmartre—the hangout of ne'er-do-wells, poets, actors, fast thinkers, fast women, and slow food (material or spiritual), which should jump off the plate into the body, as in the Italian cooking term *saltimbocco* (leap into the mouth). The front parlour, meanwhile, awaits the corpse of glib writing to be given a suitably lack-lustre dismissal.

15

CURRICULUM FOR BARDS

What kind of education does a poet need? There are as many answers to this question as there are genuine poets. Since mainstream education favours system, logic, and prose, poets as students are likely to be outsiders or written off as dreamers. The lucky ones encounter inspired teachers who sense the otherness of their longing for what Keats called "the true voice of feeling" (Gittings, *Letters*, 292) to complement the dry incisiveness of the intellect. So here is one poet's account of survival rituals.

In Virginia Woolf's novel, *To the Lighthouse*, the artist Lily Briscoe meditates on the inadequacy of language to convey precisely what one means: "No, she thought, one could say nothing to nobody. The urgency of the moment always missed its mark. Words fluttered sideways and struck the object inches too low" (240). Lily is referring to words in everyday speech; however, it is one of the achievements of verbal art, if it is any good, to correct that sideways drift—as of a wounded bird—and to wing its words towards a linguistic bullseye. Zen and the art of verbal archery.

Czeslaw Milosz, in his poem "In Milan," writes:

> I have been devouring this world in vain
> For forty years, a thousand would not be enough.
> Yes, I would like to be a poet of the senses,
> That's why I don't allow myself to become one.
> Yes, thought has less weight than the word *lemon*
> That's why in my words I do not reach for fruit.
> (*Collected Poems* 136)

Milosz does not reach for fruit, in that his zest for words is part of a fully fledged physicality that contributes to the poetic and existential meaning, rather than remaining an obtrusive gesture that could be suspected of being a frill. Kenneth Clark, in *The Nude*, writes of Rubens's nudes, whose obvious physicality never tips over into carnality: "They are grateful for life, and their gratitude spreads all through their bodies" (137). This grateful incorporation of sensuous life is also one of the touchstones of great poetry.

The practice of the "sullen craft or art" of poetry needs a counterbalance of some kind. Of all forms of physical exercise, walking seems most conducive to pondering, assimilating, and rearranging one's thoughts. Wordsworth's rolling gait as he walked was a sure-fire originator of poetic rhythms. The only time that Wordsworth shows a trace of self-deprecating humour is a passage in *The Prelude* where he describes his terrier warning him of approaching pedestrians, enabling him to desist from his mumblings and groanings as he composed. Joyce, who was novelist, musician, and poet, used to take fourteen-kilometre walks along the Seine when he was writing *Ulysses*. (Attridge 225)

Poets usually learn to camouflage their most obvious eccentricities; as Blake wrote, "I am hid." Christopher Smart used to pray in the street, for which he was locked up. Some people would like to have locked up John Betjeman, with his crushed hat, crumpled clothes, and manic laugh. The line between sanity and madness in poets is a thin one, as the Romantics knew.

Poets often defy the "norms" of conventional education. For example, they commit to memory hundreds or even thousands of lines from their favourite writers; these act as compost in the ground of their minds and refine what Eliot called the "auditory Imagination", a sophisticated awareness of the music of words, the dynamics of poetry or "the other harmony of prose."

Too little or too much. This is for every poet to wrestle with. T. S. Eliot is a great poet in spite of his formidable learning, whereas Blake could have done with more conventional discipline: one regrets that his supreme genius is not more accessible to the "common reader."

In the classical world, even solitary readers read out loud. Poets agree with this habit; the contemporary bias for silent readers makes us over-cerebral at the expense of being listeners.

An audience of one or a few is better than an abstract mass audience. Wordsworth wrote *The Prelude* to Coleridge and of course read the whole thing out loud to Coleridge, taking several days, when it was finished. But what an audience! The other listeners included the sophisticated inner ears of Dorothy and Mary Wordsworth, the Hutchinson sisters, comprising "The Gang", and Wordsworth's patrons: Sir George and Lady Beaumont.

The intellect divides, the imagination unites. "The Fall into Division, the Resurrection to Unity." (Blake)

Poetry is, in the utilitarian sense, utterly useless. But utilitarian attitudes are deplorably limited, otherwise the world would be a more just and humane place in which to live. As a young practitioner, I had to silently resist the often unspoken puritanisms: "Be a man"; "Get a decent job"; "Poetry will get you nowhere fast"; "Stop wasting your time." I wasn't wasting my time; I was just working to a different clock.

If we leave behind the limited sense of useful, we adopt a more philosophical stance enabling us to address the real issues. "What is the responsibility of the poet?" "How should a poet live?" "Why does poetry matter?" These questions can never perhaps be fully answered, but they have to be asked by those poets who take their art seriously. And the consequences of asking these questions commits the poet to a way of life: the recent majestic biography of Yeats by Roy Foster reveals the poet centrally and courageously involved in the life of his time—it is not for nothing that Yeats entitled one of his books "Responsibilities."

Poets should have carved in stone above their doorways the following quotations: "The lyf so short, the craft so long to lerne" (Chaucer); and "Bidden or unbidden, the god is always present."

Poets can never read enough; the thinness of much verse (and worse) often comes from the fact that the poet doesn't read enough of other people's work, especially that of past masters (of both genders). We have to be humbled by excellence before also being exalted by it.

Much of what we read today is superficial and lacking in nourishment. It is like fast food: it fills us temporarily but does nothing for our long-term health. Poetry is slow food; it is a meal, like the biblical loaves and fishes, which feeds us a hundred times, not just once. But this recycled food may be initially difficult for the palate to accept. In *The Western Canon*, Harold Bloom keeps going back to the strangeness of canonical works; we need tough constitutions to stomach these creations.

It doesn't much matter what kind of job a poet has as long as the art has an autonomous life of its own. Chaucer was a diplomat, Shakespeare an actor/manager, Gray a don, Eliot a banker, Wordsworth an Inspector of Stamps, Coleridge a journalist, Clare a labourer, Dickinson a professional recluse, Byron a full-time womanizer, Larkin a librarian. Poets who are teachers have taken on two very difficult arts and require complex skills in managing the demands of each one.

What is style? It is lightness of touch, what the Italians call *sprezzatura*. Bernard Maurel, an equitation expert, writes of it in terms of an achieved balance between the rider and the horse. I have substituted the word "poem" for "horse" and "poet" for "rider" in his description: "Lightness is achieved when the [poem] uses the minimum effort necessary to execute a given movement without contraction while staying supple and energetic. Lightness is judged not in terms of the comfort of the [poet] who seeks a [poem] obedient to the play of his thoughts or the lightness of his feelings, but in the resulting ease of the performance of the [poem]." Maurel sums up this quality in connection to technique: "pure

192

lightness, a technical aspect intimately linked to the accuracy of the [poem's] work."

All poets should have a pet. Smart's cat Jeoffry was an inspiring companion in the poet's madhouse years. My cat, Paddy the Celtic Tiger, fascinates me in his awareness of boundaries—to be stretched or contracted as occasion demands. He is a perfect stylist. Cowper kept madness at bay playing with Puss, Tiney, and Bess, his tame hares; King Lear's image of utter removal from community is that the little dogs—Tray, Blanche, and Sweetheart—bark at him. Byron found no-one more loyal or courageous than Boatswain, his Newfoundland dog. And he went one step further than Swift in implying humankind's Yahoodom in preferring the company of his tame bear at Cambridge and of his monkeys in Italy.

All languages are alive to the poet, especially the so-called dead ones. Poets who limit themselves to their own vernacular can never rent an apartment in the Tower of Babel, diminishing their work. There are many languages within each vernacular—dialects, "nation language," and so on. Poetry in English is greatly strengthened by the poet's acquaintance with other languages, especially those ones fertilizing the soil of English: Greek, Latin, French, German, and Italian.

Each successful poem is the elegant solution of a "problem." I use the word "elegant" in the sense that mathematicians use it—the moment when lucidity and grace come together. A perfect model for such moments is a fugue by Bach: a succinct theme is repeatedly bounced off itself in different registers or tempos, allowed to float off in expanding ripples, and finally anchored in an expressive resolution.

All poets are haunted by rhythm, whether they are musical or not. In Shakespeare's time, the rhythms of verse and music were closer together. Shakespeare must have been steeped in music, as is evident from the way he can modulate effortlessly in his plays from verse to song. Language has a music of its own, and when we approach an author, we should sound the words in our mind or read the work out aloud to taste the particular rhythms of each author. Like an actor learning a speech, this reading aloud is an excellent way of more deeply understanding the work (or the different rhythms of Shakespeare's characters). Silent reading is often too fast to allow the words to give up their depths. Slow down and allow the multiple flavours of the stew to give up their secrets.

In the search for their own voice, poets often learn more from minor or uneven writers than from their masters' voices. Philip Larkin found Yeats magnificent but too polished to learn from, selecting Hardy's countrified rhythms as more instructive. Other poets' poets are Clare and the endlessly blocked Coleridge.

Poets are, consciously or unconsciously, dedicated to the elimination of jargon. One branch of jargon is what we call buzzwords—when we ring the buzzer, we expect the door to be opened by someone in solidarity with our own ideology. In one of his most lucid essays, "The Redress of Poetry," Seamus Heaney reminds us that one of the leaders of the Easter Rising of 1916, Thomas MacDonagh, had written a book about the Elizabethan poet, Thomas Campion. And he mentions Joyce's love of Elizabethan lyrics. He continues: "Neither MacDonagh nor Joyce considered it necessary to proscribe within his reader's memory the riches of the Anglophone culture whose authority each was, in his own way, compelled to challenge." (Heaney, *Redress*, 7). In a laudable effort to redress various forms of social injustice, some writers and critics lose sight of the fact that a poem (or any true work of art) can emerge from an inequitable system and still be "a working model of inclusive consciousness." (Heaney, *Redress*, 8). If it were not, I would add, why on earth should one bother one's head about it?

In one of the greatest books ever written about sport, *Beyond a Boundary*, C. L. R. James rejoices in the superlative performances of the West Indian cricketers such as Sobers, Walcott, Weekes, and Worrell at a time when the whole population of the West Indies applauded their strokes as not just works of art, but as little blows for political freedom. James concludes his book, having described the triumph of the West Indian team, led by Worrell, in Australia; he had earlier explained his fondness for Jimmy Durante's colloquialism "That's my boy" as meaning "You're one of us." The final two sentences of the book convey a dignified celebration of self-determination while also paying tribute to the "riches of the Anglophone culture" in which James had been steeped as a youth: "Clearing their way with bat and ball, West Indians at that moment had made a public entry into the comity of nations. Thomas Arnold, Thomas Hughes and the Old Master himself [W. G. Grace] would have recognized Frank Worrell as their boy." (James 345)

A poet knows, of course, that all words are loaded. But jargon too easily aligns the writer with the "correct" ideology while often camouflaging a lack of commitment to the liberating ambiguities of language. This is using language as a steam-roller rather than a manure-spreader. Poets must be committed to the full payload of their words, or else they are impostors. The ideal poem would be like Larkin's "glass of water/Where any-angled light/ Would congregate endlessly." (Thwaite 91)

Good poets have an obsession with words amounting almost to a mania. The good poem manifests not just the approximate word, but the exactly appropriate word in the context. When we remember that there are three quarters of a million words in the complete *Oxford English Dictionary*, the choice becomes formidable. But words almost select themselves for the seasoned poet. The right word need not be a "fancy" one—one of the misconceptions of people who don't know much about poetry is that poets use "flowery" language. The opposite is true.

Litmus test for a writer's use of language: to be able to explain one's work to a Dublin pub-dweller without eliciting guffaws of derision or the glaze of incomprehension. Joyce found his basic vocabulary from following his feckless father around pubs and fishermen's cottages, or listening to his father bragging about his youthful exploits with other "chancers" like himself.

Poets have often been accused of living in "an ivory tower." A significant number of poets and writers have actually lived in towers: Yeats's medieval keep in County Galway kept him located in history and geography and provided central symbols—the tower and the winding stair; Rilke wrote his greatest poetry in a medieval tower at Müzot in Switzerland; Montaigne wrote his skeptical essays in the tower of le château de Montaigne in Périgord in southwest France; Hölderlin was assumed insane and confined in a tower at Tübingen; Clare in his incarceration described himself as living in an "English Bastille"; Gérard de Nerval compares his disinherited self to *"Le prince d'Aquitaine à la tour abolie"*; Walter Scott, whose *Ivanhoe* inspired de Nerval, built himself a Scots baronial fortress at Abbotsford, full of romantically "medieval" turrets; Jung (who mapped the psychic hinterland of poetry) built the famous tower at Bollingen as a symbolic blueprint of the psyche; Châteaubriand wrote his early work at the château de Combourg near Bordeaux; and Joyce lived briefly with Oliver St. John Gogarty (another poet) in the Martello Tower at Sandycove, one of the most famous landmarks in *Ulysses*. All of these settings are very far from ivory towers; they are places where the besieged soul of the poet can retreat into the reality of the Self, at least partly protected from the battering-rams of materialism. These places are, in short, symbolic as much as actual. Writers should choose their domiciles with care; genius is all very well, but it can only fully exfoliate when it is in tune with the *genius loci*.

E. M. Forster's formula for the good life—"Only connect"—needs to be rewritten in the light of contemporary eco-criticism: "Only interconnect."

Taking the word from music, Jung described the individuated life as an "opus." Poets are musicians in the sense that their work is often a theme, or set of themes, and variations in various mood-keys, always returning to the master key and master theme.

Poets should strive to deliver a golden and brazen world at once. Their mirror is a transforming one when they "hold it up to nature." Stanislaus Joyce writes of his brother's work: "In the mirror of his art the ugliness of the Gorgon's head may be clearly reflected, but it is cleanly severed and does not turn the beholder's heart to stone." Some writers seem intent to turn our hearts to stone.

Great poets take their metaphors from common, demotic speech. The story is told of a Shakespearean scholar walking in the fields near Stratford, coming across two countrymen working at the ancient task of reed-cutting. The professor asks them how they go about it, and one of them replies, "My mate here rough-hews them, and I shape their ends." Shakespeare "translates" these colloquialisms into Hamlet's spine-tingling lines: "There's a divinity that shapes our ends/ Rough-hew them how we will."

Poets are Prospero, Caliban, and Ariel all at once: the commanding mage, the wild man, and the airy spirit.

When Joyce was four years of age, he staged a "mystery play" for his devout parents, making sure he took the part of the Devil. No wonder his early gods were Blake and Dante.

There is an endearing story of Blake and his wife, both naked, being surprised by a visitor in their garden as they read Milton's description of Adam and Eve (out loud of course). Talk about living the part. But Blake knew what it meant to be spiritually naked.

Yeats once described the poetically immature Keats as a boy pressing his face against the window of a sweet-shop. The mature Keats, like all great poets, removes the glass: there is nothing between the reader and the "sweets" within.

Poets are translators in every sense of the word: they "carry over" in their use of metaphor; they move us from one place or condition to another (as in to "translate" a bishop); and they interpret other linguistic conventions for us. Translation in the sense of interpretation between one language and another should be part of every poet's training. Sometimes, this creates original works that stand on their own poetic feet (such as Lowell's *Imitations*.) At the very least, it enlarges the poet's vocabulary and amplifies the inner ear.

Poets are "snappers-up of unconsidered trifles." Joyce (best known for his prose, every page of which reveals the true poet and musician/composer that he also was), once told his brother that he didn't just see things, he absorbed them. Sharp details in his work, such as the snow falling on the spikes of the railings at the end of "The Dead," are not just seen, they are absorbed.

Poets are bird-watchers. Equipped with binocular vision (or, in Blake's case, quadocular vision) and an instinct for catching the joy as it flies, they allow the freedom of the skies to the creatures of their imagination but also the inviolability of their word-nests. A Zen master once tweaked a pupil's nose for saying "the birds have flown away." Birds and poems have their own autonomous lives beyond our limited perspectives.

Poets are like cooks. They change the chemistry of raw materials into a new nourishing compound. Again, it is often the small touches that reveal the master: knowing how much salt to add to the stew, or the right herb that transforms competence into brilliance.

Cultural good taste is attending a banquet of the appetites without over-eating.

16

AND JOY THE ART OF TRUE BELIEVING

"I've put those Clare books in the basement, and that's where they are going to stay." In the early 1980s, after a brief spell of teaching at a Canadian private school, I returned to the university system. My successor as Head of English at the school was overheard bragging about the above act of incarceration. Not just put away, but put down and locked up in a dark room. I don't know if that particular school has since seen the light, but "Clare in the basement" is an apt metaphor for the mainstream academic treatment of Clare, of which the most blatant is, perhaps, Jerome McGann's 1993 anthology in which Clare is poorly and misleadingly represented. In the recent reassessment of the visionary company and the welcome broadening of the canon, Clare has been almost ignored again, in spite of his genius for seeing things.

There are, happily, exceptions to this rule. In the United States, James McKusick, among others, has linked Clare to American environmentalism, and there is now a flourishing John Clare Society of North America; in Toronto, W. J. Keith and Johanne Clare have been strong advocates of Clare's work; in Ireland, John MacKenna—author of

Clare: a Novel—has reinforced my view that Clare's work is little known, in spite of the fact that many contemporary Irish poets—Seamus Heaney and Michael Longley among them—have, since the sixties, regarded Clare as a poetic icon. Clare's work, then, is beginning to cross more than one national border, albeit at a snail's pace. Here in England, very properly, Clare's work has rapidly gained momentum, so that by 1994 John Goodridge was able to report that Clare had suddenly appeared on everyone's agenda. And today's gathering amply demonstrates Clare's diverse appeal, his ability to cross barriers of language, nationality, gender, and discipline. In my paper, I want to move the discussion from literal borders to artistic frontiers; I want to examine the theme of pleasure and joy in Clare's work, and demonstrate that these words constitute for Clare a radical aesthetic, enabling him to move from alienation to communal values in contact with natural energies.

In a judicious poem about Clare called "'Sorrowful, Yet Always Rejoicing' Vincent," Norman Iles writes:

> Odd that 'sad'
> Rhymes with 'glad';
> And both with 'mad'.
> (Goodridge, 1994, 58)

Clare was destined to live out Wordsworth's gloomy assessment of the Romantic temperament: "We poets in our youth begin in gladness,/But thereof comes in the end despondency and madness." (Wu 531). Clare himself was well aware of the two sides of this tragic coin: "The brighter the sun beam the deeper the shadow", he writes in a fragment. (Robinson et al. *Middle Period* II, 13). One could start a poem similar to Iles's with another cluster of rhymes reflecting some of Clare's obsessions:

> Odd that 'boys'
> Rhymes with 'joys'
> And both with 'noise.'
> Sometimes with 'voice';
> Also with 'toys'
> And with 'destroys.'

Four of the above rhymes occur in "Birds Nesting," a masterpiece from Volume II of *Poems of the Middle Period*. Clare's "voice", one could say, lies between "joys" and "destroys."

These rhymes and other similar clusters are, of course, littered throughout Clare's work; Clare was sufficiently indebted to the oral tradition to know that incremental repetition can be a virtue. It is worth lingering over these rhymes a little to examine their implications. First, joy is short-lived and fragile. Second, joy is sometimes associated with an escape from danger. Third, Clare is honest in associating pleasure and joy in connection with illicit or mischievous activities; the countless boys roaming the countryside in his work are not just innocent bird-watchers: they are engaged in a hunt, where anticipation of the prize is as important as the prize itself:

> The schoolboys peep in every bush
> & eager as for money stoop
> To hunt the grass & bunch of rush
> Where ever birds are startled up
> The Pewet wakes their eager joys
> The moor & meadows noisey guest

Where ever birds but make a noise
Anticipation sees a nest
(Robinson et al. *Middle Period* II, 163)

One is reminded of the modern colloquial usage "joy-ride,"
which originally meant stealing someone else's car and going
for a spin. The same blend of anticipation, fear, and furtive
pleasure is present in Clare's actual and imaginative acts of
trespass, which, for the self-taught poet, are joy-rides into
forbidden territory. As other critics have noted, Clare is
close here to the young Wordsworth as described in the early
books of *The Prelude*. Wordsworth kills off this mischievous
owl-echoing boy at the end of "There was a boy . . . ". Clare,
however, keeps this boy alive in his work: " 'Cuck cuck' it
cries & mocking boys/Crie 'cuck' & still it stutters more"
(Robinson et al. *Middle Period* II, 183). By such means, a
characteristic see-saw of emotion is created—"I see" and "I
saw" become almost interchangeable.

But Clare the hunting boy is also on the trail of a different
quarry, and in this aesthetic world joy is also a crucial word.
Inspiration seems to be intimately connected to the art of
listening: "There is a voice thats heard & felt & seen" he
writes of the "language wrote on earth & sky", where the
auditory and tactile words precede the visual (Robinson et
al. *Middle Period* II, 212). Walter Ong reminds us in *Orality
and Literacy* that "sight isolates, sound incorporates." (72).
When Clare writes later in the same poem: "I read its language & its speech is joy", the reading involved is not just
a linear, cognitive one but a joyously attentive act of listening (Robinson et al. *Middle Period* II, 213). It is as if Clare
is echolocating himself in both the actual and the cultural
landscape, as he catches echoes of nature's voice as well as
echoes of his own extensive reading in the poetic tradition.

In fact, where a formally educated poet is likely to encounter blockage when confronted with the burden of the past, Clare often crosses this frontier with surprising ease, with a sense of belonging to an immortal freemasonry rather than working under an anxiety of influence:

> An image to the mind is brought
> Where happiness enjoys
> An easy thoughtlessness of thought
> & meets excess of joys
> (Robinson et al. *Middle Period* III, 582)

Clare also refuses to be overawed by classical mythology: " I have been teribly plagued with the muses since I saw you I think I have wrote 50 Sonnets—wether they are inspired by those ladys I cant [say]", he writes in a letter. And in another letter, he refers to his "old rawbone hack of a pegasus"—obviously not a thoroughbred—and he has little trouble domesticating it: "you have clapt a spur to old Peggy which starts her off agen at full trott" (Storey 13, 28, 29). One could say that Clare had too many burdens in the present to be bothered by the burdens of the past.

I don't want for a moment to give the impression that I am ignoring Clare's very real suffering; the dark of his life, however, is woven into the light: "Suffering, but always rejoicing". As many readers have noted, the miracle of Clare's work is precisely this blend: just as James Hessey on a visit to the Clare country could only see flat unpromising terrain, the reader or critic who exclusively stresses the harsh facts of Clare's life does the transforming artistry of Clare's work a disservice. The fact is, Clare finds more than a convenient necklace of rhymes in the word "joy"; he finds one of his major themes. In doing so, he is close to the ideal poet as described in the Preface to *Lyrical Ballads*. The poet, writes Wordsworth, is one in tune with "the grand elementary principle of pleasure." This pleasure constitutes "the native and naked dignity of man," and is a principle by which "he knows, and feels, and lives, and moves." (Wu 527)

In a remarkable essay, "The Fate of Pleasure," Lionel Trilling describes that passage as "bold to the point of being shocking" in that it echoes and reorients St. Paul's statement that we "live, and move, and have our being" in God. Notice that Wordsworth's first verb is "knows": pleasure, for Wordsworth, is a form of knowledge. Trilling goes on to demonstrate that pleasure in the Wordsworthian sense has had a thin time of it in post-1950 mainstream literature (his essay dates from the early sixties). Much of modern literature, according to Trilling, is dedicated to the principle of "unpleasure" and sees as part of its task the destruction of "specious good" (Frye 73-106). One only has to think of the fate of words such as "dilettante" and "amateur" and "aesthete," all originally honorific words, to remember the wariness modern culture exhibits towards such concepts.

When people today think of the word "pleasure," they are likely to associate it with some form of self-indulgence, or at least with trivial activities. But this is far from the meaning intended by Wordsworth, Keats, and Clare. The best explication of this difference is by M. L. Rosenthal in his Introduction to a discussion of Yeats's technique in *Running to Paradise: Yeats's Poetic Art*:

"The 'pleasure' in question—the special pleasure of art—includes much more than the sunny or voluptuous poems of unalloyed joy that might at first come to mind. It extends to work that is elegiac, tragic, bitterly witty, or even grossly

disagreeable. It does not depend on the reflection of conge-
nial attitudes. Rather, it is a matter of felicitous craftsman-
ship at the service of a work's inner structure of feeling and
discovery." (xii)

With this definition in mind, we can ask what is the fate of
pleasure in Clare's work?

For Clare, as for Wordsworth, pleasure and joy are forms of
knowledge:

> I read its language & its speech is joy
> So without teaching when a lonely boy
> Each weed to me did happy tidings bring
> Plain as the daisey wrote the name of spring
> (Robinson et al. *Middle Period* II, 213)

Again, just as Wordsworth associates "bliss" with the "inward eye" in "The Daffodils," Clare uses the word "inward"
to imply that joy is not just intense pleasure; it is a different
order of being altogether: "Ive felt a pleasure aye an inward
joy" he begins in the poem "Gathering Wild Flowers." (Robinson et al. *Middle Period* II, 289). And poetry/poesy/posy
is always associated with joy. His initiation into poetry, as
he opened Thomson's *The Seasons*, "made[his] heart twitter
with joy" (Robinson and Powell, *By Himself,* 10), and from
then on poesy's "dwelling joy/ Of humble quietness" continues to triumph over all. Joy almost chokes the little throat of
the robin as he "trembles oer his under notes" and sings his
"under song/In joys own cue" (Robinson et al. *Middle Period*
III, 584,535, 534).

This under-song of nature's poetry is one in which instinct
is allied to taste:

Taste with as many hues doth hearts engage
As leaves & flowers do upon natures page
Not mind alone the instinctive mood declares
But birds & flowers & insects are its heirs
Taste is their joyous heritage & they
All choose for joy in a peculiar way
(Robinson et al. *Middle Period* III, 303)

A little later in this poem, "Shadows of Taste," Clare reverses the normal assumptions of so-called enlightened man: the shepherd "with unlearned ken" wonders at the "learned marks" of the yellow-hammer, and "Finds strange eggs scribbled as with ink & pen" (Robinson et al. *Middle Period* III, 304). In the words of another poem, the child wonders "That birds who served no prentiseship/ Could build their nests so well" (Robinson et al. *Middle Period* III, 242). In Irish mythology, Oisin argues for the joyous artistry of nature against the encroaching rule of Saint Patrick: "Don't they make their nests very nice, and they never got any instruction or teaching from God?" (McDiarmid and Waters 160). Both Clare and Oisin suggest that we learn our trade from the humblest creatures.

The kind of taste emerging from these quotations is very different from that so fascinatingly exposed by John Brewer in *The Pleasures of the Imagination*, of which one reviewer wrote: "The great lesson taught here is that the new art forms [of the eighteenth century] were all entangled with money, sex, and social pretension." Clare's art, with its lack of consumerism, its ability to be "lord of that it does not possess," in Edward Thomas's fine phrase, is closer to what Canadian First Nations people call "indigenous theology." Clare may be slow in reaching readers in other English-speaking countries, but his themes are a natural passport to the hearts of indigenous people. Four years ago, I had the privilege of teaching in a First Nations programme; Clare struck an immediate chord with my students. One of the students, Jill Harris, Chief of the Penelakut Tribe, told me of her researches into the settlement of the tidal marsh on the Saanich Peninsula near Victoria. This marsh had for centuries been a sustainable ecosystem whose indigenous inhabitants regarded it as a gift from the Creator, their responsibility being to sustain its resources. Within a short period after settlement, the marsh was drained, the lands enclosed, the reeds and wildlife destroyed, the people put on a reserve, their artefacts confiscated and sold to museums, and their children torn from their parents and sent to residential schools. At the centre of this site, all that remains from the ravages of what Clare calls this "buonaparte" is a sacred spring with very cold, pure water, still used for vision quests—rites of initiation. Jill told me that the last time she was there, a friend of hers said: "We have to sneak in here now." Trespass again. The parallels are too striking to need spelling out—when I quoted some of the enclosure elegies to Jill, she smiled in sad recognition:

> 'Look backward on the days of yore
>   'Upon my injur'd brook
> 'In fancy con its Beauties o'er
>   'How it had us'd to look
> 'O then what trees my banks did crown
>   'What Willows flourishd here
> 'Hard as the ax that Cut them down
>   'The senceless wretches were'
> (Robinson and Powell, *Early Poems* I, 233)

Clare can hardly be accused of indulging in "specious good," yet I believe his aesthetic sense is as fine as any of the poets he admired. Wordsworth once told Charles James Fox that he wanted his work to illustrate that "men who do not wear fine clothes can feel deeply." (Wu 512). Clare not only feels deeply but finely and comprehensively. His work is elementary in the best sense, just as it is pedestrian in the best sense; it brings us to our senses in every sense of the word. His link with green Romanticism and indigenous cultures reminds us how urgently we need this "ecological minstrel," in Richard Mabey's phrase (Goodridge, 1995, 6). Mabey and Jonathan Bate have both compared Clare's incantations to aboriginal song-lines, and David Rothenberg in *Why Birds Sing: A Journey into the Mystery of Bird Song* praises Clare's scientifically artful transcription of the nightingale's song. Clare's ability to move through a landscape without imposing himself on it links him also to medieval anonymities.

Clare gives us verbal mastery and sensory nutrition in a way we get from few other writers. He may have chafed at his status as a "clown," as he calls himself, but he suspects that there is no singing school, no curriculum for bards, even for the privileged poet. The singing-masters of his soul are not only the monuments of unageing intellect— the bards—but the birds whose eggs he had once hunted and whose songs are for him paradigms of art. And this blend of mind and nature is always joyful, whole, and expansive: "Her joys are ever green her world is wide" (Robinson et al. *Middle Period* III, 458). Art is a joyous creed that escapes the fundamentalism of the intellect or spirit in isolation: "& joy the art of true believing" (Robinson et al. *Middle Period* IV, 118). Our rational tradition has separated joy and art and belief; for Clare, they are inseparable, or they were before decay set in. In this way, I claim, Clare rescues pleasure from its fate in the late eighteenth century and, indeed, at the beginning of the twenty-first century. He redefines for us the relevance of the beautiful. That is why he is, in the words of the 1802 Preface to *Lyrical Ballads*, a "rock of defence of human nature; an upholder and preserver, carrying every where with him relationship and love." (Bloom and Trilling 604)

For all his material deprivations, Clare never doubts the autonomy of poetry: for him, it is a "self creating joy" (Robinson et al. *Middle Period* III, 582). This links him to the other Romantics: "The Genius of Poetry must work out its own salvation in a man: It cannot be matured by law & precept, but by sensation & watchfulness in itself—That which is creative must create itself" writes Keats (Gittings, *Letters*, 156). It links him also to ancient traditions concerning the mysterious origins of poetry: the bard Phemius in *The Odyssey* says: "I had no teacher but myself" (Rieu 339). Clare's *ars poetica*, like Horace's, has plenty of *dulce* along with the *utile*. And Heaney in *The Redress of Poetry* writes: "Poetry cannot afford to lose its fundamentally self-delighting inventiveness, its joy in being a process of language as well as a representation of things in the world." (5). No matter how much we may anticipate it, we are always, it seems, surprised by joy. This talent for being surprised, and hence self-created, seems to be a constant with Clare; if luck favours the prepared mind, Clare is both a learned and a lucky poet: he has done his homework, and so is able, in Pope's words, to "*snatch a Grace* beyond the Reach of Art." (Butt 149). He is a model, not just for self-taught poets, but for every poet, for all poets have to look into their hearts and write.

In my book *John Clare and Picturesque Landscape* (Oxford 1983), I attempted to show how Clare turns the language of landscape on its head. In this paper, I have discussed his unique pleasure principle as a way of re-placing ourselves. I believe we can rescue Clare from the basement, that dark room where his negative image awaits developing so we can see the whole picture. Clare speaks to our present condition in that he makes a lamentation for a lost world the opportunity for the joyful reintegration of our unpersonified selves. He impels us to make our own vision quest, our own initiation into a visionary company that is a true community. This quintessentially parochial poet turns out to have taken the world as his parish.

17

THE WEIGHT OF TOO MUCH LIBERTY

How can you have too much liberty, you might ask? Indeed, in the political sphere, there is almost always too little of it, and the good citizen in me deplores that. But the artist in me knows what Wordsworth means in his sonnet about the sonnet when he writes of "the weight of too much liberty." Here is the sonnet:

> Nuns fret not at their Convent's narrow room;
> And Hermits are contented with their Cells;
> And Students with their pensive Citadels;
> Maids at the Wheel, the Weaver at his Loom,
> Sit blithe and happy; Bees that soar for bloom
> High as the highest Peak of Furness Fells,
> Will murmur by the hour in Foxglove bells:
> In truth, the prison, unto which we doom
> Ourselves, no prison is: and hence to me,
> In sundry moods, 'twas pastime to be bound
> Within the Sonnet's scanty plot of ground:
> Pleased if some Souls (for such there needs must be)
> Who have felt the weight of too much liberty,
> Should find brief solace there, as I have found.
> (Gill 286)

For me, the creation of a work of art is a weighty responsibility enough without having to strive to be original. Why not, says my inner voice, stand on the shoulders of my predecessors? If my work fails to fly, I can sink back on their comforting torso, like a child piggy-backing on Dad's shoulders. For most of the time, of course, our work does fail to fly. It is weighed down with the concerns of this world, with (to use another Wordsworth line) "the weary weight of all this unintelligible world." We are artistically bound by gravity as much as physically. The art is too much with us. Why not cut the traces and float off into the freedom of space? Well, easier said than done. Dream on, as we say, and this is the stuff that dreams are made on.

In the art of carpentry, there is an adage: "Measure twice, cut once." If we apply this to any art, it means that most of the time, we are preoccupied with the practical demands of the activity, whether it be cleaning brushes, practicing scales, or counting syllables. If we do these rituals often enough, we reach a point where a trance-like state of dynamic alertness takes over, and we are operating on another level of consciousness. If you are a Freudian, you call this "communing with one's inner child," if you are a Jungian, you are accessing the collective unconscious, if you are religious, you have been ravished by the Holy Ghost, if you are an ancient Greek or Roman, your Muse has knocked on the door or your daimon has awoken from slumber. Whatever you call it, I believe that it appears fleetingly and sporadically, and must be cajoled and enticed with constant ritual. Modern educated minds don't like the word "irrational," but another way of describing the experience is that the mind transcends the rational and enters a realm of creative uncertainty, of fruitful contradiction, of what the mystics have called "daz-zling darkness."

Where does form come into all this? For me, form is a given, it is where we start. It is our inheritance, our artistic DNA. It is what Goethe in *Faust* described as "Shaping, reshaping, / The eternal mind's eternal pastime." Form is the given that "Can always be reimagined," in Heaney's words, "however four-square,/ Plank-thick, hull-stupid and out of its time/ It happens to be." (*Seeing Things* 29). There is, I believe, a mis-taken direction in the practice and theory of many art forms in recent decades, which pooh-poohs formalities and stress-es authentic emotion. Put yourself in the right mood, these theories seem to say, and you will create authentic work. But this so often leads only to banality. As the contemporary American poet, Mary Oliver, puts it in *Rules for the Dance*: "Emotion does not elicit feeling. Style elicits feeling" (96). The acquisition of style requires a humble immersion in the traditional wisdom of one's chosen art, a constant emula-tion of the best models, a relentless repetition of the most memorable utterances. Only in this way can psychic forces burst to the surface without causing actual damage. All this is rooted in contradiction; the rational mind cannot bear contradiction—one thought annihilates another opposing thought. But art of any depth thrives on contradiction, just as religious tradition does. Form acts as a kind of beneficent drug that enables us to transcend the ego and rationality. It carries the weight of our thoughts like the strainer arches of a Gothic cathedral, so that we can soar while still connected to the earth.

Let's now look at a specific form: the couplet. The couplet, like the sonnet, is an invention of the Middle Ages. In Eng-lish, the form was first used, and brilliantly, by Chaucer.

Perhaps my favourite passage in all of English literature is Chaucer's homage to the humble daisy in The Prologue to the *Legend of Good Women*:

> Now have I thanne eek this condicioun,
> That, of al the floures in the mede,
> Thanne love I most thise floures white and rede,
> Swiche as men callen daysyes in our toun.
> To hem have I so gret affeccioun,
> As I seyde erst, whanne comen is the May,
> That in my bed ther daweth me no day
> That I nam up and walkyng in the mede
> To seen this flour ayein the sonne sprede,
> Whan it upryseth erly by the morwe.
> That blisful sighte softneth al my sorwe,
> So glad am I, whan that I have presence
> Of it, to doon it alle reverence,
> As she that is of alle floures flour,
> Fulfilled of al vertu and honour,
> And evere ilyke faire, and fressh of hewe;
> And I love it, and ever ylike newe,
> And evere shal, til that myn herte dye.
> Al swere I nat, of this I wol nat lye;
> Ther loved no wight hotter in his lyve,
> And whan that hit ys eve, I renne blyve,
> As sone as evere the sonne gynneth weste,
> To seen this flour, how it wol go to reste,
> For fere of nyght, so hateth she derknesse.
> (Robinson F. N. 483)

The couplet should sound its chimes almost inaudibly. At times, though, the rhymes ram the meaning home with a definitive straight to the jaw, as in the clinching lines of the English sonnet:

> If this be error and upon me proved,
> I never writ, nor no man ever loved.
> (Sonnet 116)

And it sets its seal on the mostly blank-verse speeches of Shakespeare's drama, niftily summing up an act or a scene:

> Our hands are full of business; let's away.
> Advantage feeds him fat while men delay.
> (*Henry IV, Part One*, 3, 2)

Alexander Pope brought the formal, or heroic couplet, to perfection in the early eighteenth century. My English professor at Trinity College, Dublin once asked the class to look out the window, and notice how the four classical columns of the Chapel matched the four classical columns of the Examination Hall, and how these buildings were the terminus of ten spaced doorways, broken only by the larger Front Gate. He then returned us to our text by Pope, pointing out the rhymes of the couplet as the terminating buildings and the ten syllables echoing the ten doorways, the pregnant pause of the mid-line comma functioning like the Front Gate. There are people who call this kind of thing quaint, but Trinity's Front Square is as much a representative product of early- to mid-eighteenth culture as Pope's work. One is tempted to ask: Does our urban/suburban sprawl echo the formlessness of modern verse? And is a return to form a regressive step, a nostalgia for an outworn paradigm? As Trummy Young, Louis Armstrong's trombonist, used to sing: "It ain't what you do, it's the way how you do it." To be truly original, after all, is to return to the origins. There are certain forms that seem to be inexhaustible and inexhaustibly fecund: they keep extemporizing like those slow-motion movie sequences of opening blossoms. It seems that, at this moment in history, to return to form is a dynamically progressive step. Poets of Canada, unite—you have nothing to lose but your weight.

Pope's range is vast, from the cosmic chutzpah of

> Nature, and Nature's Laws lay hid in Night.
> God said, *Let Newton be!* and All was *Light*.
> (Butt 808)

to the verbal waltz of

> True Ease in Writing comes from Art, not Chance,
> As those move easiest who have learn'd to dance.
> (155)

to the colloquial contempt of

> Go teach Eternal Wisdom how to rule—
> Then drop into thyself, and be a fool!
> (517)

And Pope could be describing modern academe when he writes:

> A Lumberhouse of books in ev'ry head,
> For ever reading, never to be read!
> (759)

The other great strength of the form is that it is written in iambic pentameter (five beats, ten syllables per line). The ten-syllable line is one of the cornerstones of English poetry, perhaps the most important one. It echoes ordinary speech. Listen to the following:

I think he's putting on a lot of weight. (10 syllables)

You get the apples, and I'll get the pears. (10 syllables)

Did you ever hear such a silly thing? (10 syllables)

Shall I compare thee to a summer's day? (Sonnet 18)

Put out the light, and then put out the light. (*Othello*)

And Holdfast is the only dog, my duck . . . (*Henry V*)

How easy doth thou take all England up . . . (*King John*)

Never, never, never, never, never. (*King Lear*)

Variants of nine or eleven syllables occur quite frequently. Shakespeare's most famous line is actually eleven syllables:

To be or not to be, that is the ques-tion.

The out-of-kilter quality of this line is entirely appropriate for the tortured soliloquy it introduces. And the actor playing Richard the Third sometimes stresses the extra syllable in the word determined, making the line as hump-backed as Richard himself:

I am determin-ed to prove a villain.

Sometimes the ten or eleven syllables contain some pithy

dialogue, as in the following from *King John*, which in the text is spaced out over five lines:

Death/ My Lord?/A grave/He shall not live/Enough.

This is the heartbeat of English. Like a snowflake, the underlying structure would seem monotonous, yet it is never the same. Never, never, never, never, never.

Equipped with this subtle architectural invention, poets ancient and modern can put in place the weightiest rocks or the flimsiest meringues of meaning. Contrary to the expectations of those who believe form to be a kind of prison, it energises the Houdini poets to break its padlocks. Unlike the physical constraints of real life, the Bastille of form liberates its happy prisoners; its service is perfect freedom:

True Wit is Nature to Advantage drest,
What oft was Thought, but ne'er so well Exprest.
(Butt 153)

Finally, a word about my poem "James Clarence Mangan in Trinity College Library." Although about an Irish subject, it was written in Toronto in 1972, and is one of that growing number of poems written by exiles acquiring a double vision as they look back to the mother country from the step-country. James Clarence Mangan is a minor Irish icon, little known outside the country except to scholars. He was an Irish example of the nineteenth-century Bohemian artist, dubbed by Baudelaire *"poètes maudits"*—accursed poets. In the context of the poem, Mangan represents the frustrated marginalized voice of the native tradition (he made famous translations from the Gaelic) as he works at a mundane job amidst the splendours of the Trinity Library, then, as now,

219

lined with busts of famous men, including three great Irishmen of the eighteenth century—Swift, Burke, and Berkeley. The Long Room at Trinity is one of the most thrilling spaces I know, not least because of the complexities of Irish history. Among various classical worthies, for example, one comes across a bust of Robert Emmet, the Trinity graduate hanged for Ireland in 1803. I think also of the two graduate brothers hanged together in 1798 as they held hands. Swift, Burke, and Berkeley represent that proud tradition called the Middle Nation—those usually non-Catholic Irishmen educated in an Anglo tradition, but with a deep love for Ireland. This was a dangerous and divided stance, and it probably contributed to Swift's mental instability.

Formally, I try to combine a colloquial, narrative voice within a loose flowing couplet structure; while the meaning runs from couplet to couplet in the main body of the poem, the final two lines are more akin to the end-stopped, self-contained heroic couplet. The final lines are thus read much more slowly:

> His weary eyes watch lanterns in the square
> Squeak in wind, papers blown about the air,
>
> Great trees dishevelled by the sudden squall,
> Which woke him from his dream behind the wall
>
> Of books, bound books that he knows little of
> Except the few that fire his frenzied love
>
> And keep him from his cataloguer's task,
> (And like the busts, his face a pallid mask).

The snug alcove where he preferred to work
Was near the sightless gaze of Swift and Burke,

But his rage was of other kind than theirs.
Stiffened with alcohol, he sought the stairs

And stumbled out of eighteenth-century grace,
Across the cobbles, dreaming of a race

As yet unborn, or dead so long he saw
The merest ghosts emerge from history's maw,

And racked by drugs and dreams, like Baudelaire,
He walked the city of his heart's despair,

Across the river, up to his dark den,
And lit his candle, coughed, took up his pen

And wrote some verse that morning would not spare
(The pale sky showed the dawn already there)

Until, defeated, he snuffed out the flame
And with it seemed to blow away his fame.

Tomorrow, Berkeley, Swift, glue, ink, and dust,
And madness winking at him from a bust.
(Brownlow 93-4)

18

FIELDWORK

In the landscape of English literature, there are many different sorts of terrain, many fields of force, some of them hedged, ditched, and cultivated to within an inch of their lives. The map of this country of the mind has been extensively charted, plotted, and contoured, so that the lie of the land is familiar to readers and scholars. Signposts point the way, the most common trees and flowers have been classified and labelled, passable roads or lanes lead in more or less straight lines though the territory. But what is that ragged-looking patch of land over there, with no obvious signposts, no discernable pathways, no hedges and ditches?

> The sleety winds fondle the rushy beards of Shancoduff
> While the cattle-drovers sheltering in the Featherna
>   Bush
> Look up and say:"Who owns them hungry hills
> That the water-hen and snipe must have forsaken?
> A poet? Then by heavens he must be poor."
> I hear and is my heart not badly shaken?
> (Kavanagh 30)

Patrick Kavanagh, who wrote these lines in 1934 about his

native County Monaghan in Ireland, is Ireland's best-loved poet along with Yeats and Heaney. Kavanagh stands in relation to the great W. B. Yeats in much the same way that John Clare stands to his great contemporary William Wordsworth. While Wordsworth and Yeats stride the high road of Romanticism and Modernism respectively, Clare and Kavanagh work off the beaten track, exploring the by-paths, beating the bounds of their parishes and beyond to where cultivated land shades off into heath, marsh, bog, and fenland.

No one was ever more attached to his locality than John Clare. In his prose autobiographical fragments he describes a childhood ramble that brought him into disturbingly unknown territory: "so I eagerly wanderd on and rambled among the furze the whole day till I got out of my knowledge when the very wild flowers and birds seemd to forget me and I imagind they were the inhabitants of new countrys the very sun seemd to be a new one and shining in a different quarter of the sky" (Robinson and Powell, *Clare by Himself*, 40-41). Clare's imagination gave to everything he knew a local habitation and a name, so much so that a walk of ten miles or so could radically disorient him, could plunge him into a distanced frame of mind, could, as we say, alienate him. Clare's radical alienation from his local Eden prefigures our own expulsion from the garden of earthly delights, from a whole and wholesome involvement in an animated environment. We, too, are out of our knowledge.

Clare's fieldwork has many dimensions. For a start, he was literally a fieldworker, a day-labourer eking out a marginal existence from the land; second, he was a fieldworker in the scientific sense, a field-naturalist, becoming a self-taught ornithologist and botanist whose extensive knowledge was used in the compilation of contemporary publications, some of which are still current and accurate today. For example, of the one hundred and forty-five wild birds that Clare knew from personal observation, sixty-five are first recorded in his work; third, he cultivated his chosen field of poetry with the greatest care, reading the classics of literature with as much relish as he recited and played on his fiddle hundreds of local ballads and songs. In Clare's local dialect, that of the borders of Northamptonshire and Cambridgeshire, the word "posey" meant poetry as well as a bunch of flowers—so Clare calls his greatest manuscript volume "The Midsummer Cushion," a collection particularly rich in sonnets, thus linking the poet's assembling of poems to the local tradition of putting a posy of flowers in the cottage window at the height of summer.

The fields themselves around Clare's boyhood village underwent a massive historical change in his youth. The enclosure of fields had been sporadically going on since medieval times, but, in response to the pressures of the Napoleonic Wars, when England had to feed itself, parliament authorized widespread enclosure policies. The flattish countryside around Helpston, Clare's village, then in Northamptonshire, now in Cambridgeshire, had remained much as it was for centuries. But in 1809, when Clare was sixteen, hordes of surveyors appeared in the landscape of Clare's boyhood, intent on carving it up into more manageable and efficient segments: "These paths are stopt—the rude philistines thrall/Is laid upon them & destroyed them all/Each little tyrant with his little sign" (Robinson et al. *Middle Period* II, 349). One result of this process was the disappearance of much of the semi-wild common lands around the village, on which even the poorest villagers could keep hens or a cow or a donkey. The modern world, with its economic imperatives, its bureaucrats with little feeling for autonomous localities, and its intensified class divisions took up lodging in Clare's village; he hated it:

> Inclosure came & trampled on the grave
> Of labours rights & left the poor a slave
> (Robinson et al. *Middle Period* II, 348)

Clare, who at an early age had discovered that he had no prospects—either material or topographical—now had to take his botanising walks in a landscape bristling with menace. Even Wordsworth and Coleridge, on their moon-gazing rambles in Somerset, were once reported to the authorities as suspected French spies. What chance did the "peasant poet" have of escaping suspicion, as he wandered the countryside associating with gypsies, playing his fiddle at local dances, and prying into nature's secret places in search of nightingales' nests? No wonder he identified with moles, those inoffensive creatures whose little molehills he climbed in delicious parody of the poets and tourists climbing their hills in search of prospects and picturesque vistas. Now, wherever Clare went, he was likely to be trespassing, just as a boy he had hopped over the estate wall of Burghley Park, home of the Marquess of Exeter, to read a volume of Thomson's poetry he had just bought at Stamford. The innocent landscape of Clare's boyhood was now a minefield of potential transgression, analogous to the literary tradition of educated folk into which he longed to make articulate raids.

There is, I believe, a strong correlation between Clare's actual landscape and his literary landscape. Just as the former was surveyed and enclosed, the latter was tidied up by Clare's conventionally educated editors. Clare resisted unnecessary punctuation as much as he hated enclosure. Although he usually had to give in to educated opinion that his work was wild and unkempt, he resented the clipping of his syntactical wings. The debate continues today: whether to publish Clare in what is now known as the "primitive" editorial style with the poems and prose presented exactly as they appear in Clare's manuscripts, or to allow editors to impose their own standards of orthodoxy as regards spelling, punctuation, and dialect. A third option has been recently promulgated by Jonathan Bate, Clare's finest biographer, in adopting a middle ground of light punctuation for the sake of clarity and readability, but eschewing further interference. I have much sympathy with Bate's position, and there is evidence that Clare would have endorsed it, but I want to emphasize how complex this question is.

In her recent amusing book on punctuation, *Eats, Shoots and Leaves,* Lynne Truss reminds us that the placing of a single comma can wreak havoc with intended meaning. If Protestants want to get into heaven, they will punctuate the following passage thus:

I say unto thee, this day thou shalt be with me in Paradise.

Catholics, however, who believe in Purgatory, punctuate thus:

I say unto thee this day, thou shalt be with me in Paradise. (74)

As a good Anglican schoolboy, I remember thinking: "That's nice, the crucified thief will be in heaven by dinner-time." But the Catholic version implies: "Hold on, when you shuffle off this mortal coil, you'll have a lot of explaining to do first."

It is not just a matter of punctuation. Clare's work is a veritable hotchpotch of differing and often competing styles. There is the local dialect of a native son of the East Midlands; there is the folklore and balladry passed down for centuries in his locality; there is the literary language acquired in Clare's extensive reading, abounding in archaisms and Spenserian imagery largely abandoned by cosmopolitan contemporary writers; there is the scientific exactitude of Clare's botanical and ornithological knowledge; there is Clare's delight in onomatopeic invention, as when he attempts to transcribe the song of the nightingale. Traditionally, it went "jug, jug, jug" as in "The Waste Land"; Clare writes:

> She'd scarce repeat the note again
> —'Chew-chew chew-chew' & higher still
> Cheer-cheer cheer-cheer more loud & shrill
> 'Cheer-up cheer-up cheer-up'—& dropt
> Low 'Tweet tweet jug jug jug' & stopt
> One moment just to drink the sound
> Her music made & then a round
> Of stranger witching notes was heard
> As if it was a stranger bird
> 'Wew-wew wew-wew chur-chur chur-chur
> 'Woo-it woo-it'—could this be her
> 'Tee-rew tee-rew tee-rew tee-rew
> 'Chew-rit chew-rit'—& ever new
> 'Will-will will-will grig-grig grig-grig'
> The boy stopt sudden on the brig
> To hear the 'tweet tweet tweet' so shrill
> Then 'jug jug jug' & all was still
> (Robinson et al. *Middle Period* III, 500)

You might say that this goes beyond the limits of intelligible language, but James Joyce would have sympathized. Here is a passage from *Finnegans Wake*: "We are now diffusing among our lovers of this sequence (to you! to you!) the dewfolded song of the naughingels (Alys! Alysaloe!) from their sheltered positions, in rosescenery haydyng, sweetishsad lightandgayle twittwin twosingwoolow." (359-360)

The comparison may seem almost shocking. Joyce, as modern scholars tell us, is an intellectual giant, and guaranteed to keep the Ph. D. industry going for another fifty years. Clare, on the other hand, as the same scholars tell us, is of scant intellectual interest (besides, he couldn't spell), lacking the philosophical cement that might have made his scattered perceptions more respectable. If only he had been educated, he might have been able to articulate his vision to our satisfaction (and given us more topics with which to conference-hop). But lovers and scholars of Clare's work, who are often poets themselves, and among whom are several contemporary Irish writers, say: "Wait a minute, Clare may sometimes be incoherent, but are the following qualifications not arresting? One, he occupies a unique social and historical niche; two, he is the greatest writer of a totally vanished rural past; three, he fused scientific exactitude with poetic imagery; four, he is the first most authentic voice of ecopoetics, the first chronicler of a disappearing and lost landscape and voiceless people, animals, and birds; five, he invents a new mode of perception, not through ignorance, but by largely ignoring the constraints of standard grammar and punctuation." And so we have been saying for forty years; there is now grudging acknowledgement of his achievement, but Clare is not yet firmly ensconced in the literary canon.

The sonnet was one of Clare's favourite forms: he wrote

hundreds of them, some mere exercises, others little gems unlike anything else in English literature. I want now to attempt an analysis of this uniqueness, hoping to show that it goes beyond punctuation or the lack of it. Clare's sonnets, I believe, are the product of an idiosyncratic vision of startling originality. Having to choose between them, one feels like a child walking on a beach particularly rich in seashells—few of them perfect, perhaps, but all temptingly different.

The sonnet has fascinated writers since its invention. It comes trailing clouds of glory: a form that Spenser, Donne, Shakespeare, Milton, and Wordsworth have wrought into sonorous presence is hardly one to take up lightly. And yet, many lesser fry insist on doing so. Wordsworth describes the sonnet as follows: "Instead of looking at this composition as a piece of architecture, making a whole out of three parts, I have been much in the habit of preferring the image of an orbicular body,—a sphere—or a dew-drop." (*The Letters of William and Dorothy Wordsworth: The Later Years.* Oxford, 1939, II, 653). Here, Wordsworth shows his Romantic credentials: he prefers using an organic, natural metaphor to an architectural one. In doing so, he comes close, I believe, to describing the kind of sonnet Clare excels at. But let us remind ourselves of how different this verbal dew-drop is compared to the usual sonnet.

One critic convincingly compares the traditional sonnet to the sonata form in music. The sonata was brought mozartfully to perfection by composers such as Haydn and Mozart in the eighteenth century. It has three clear parts: Statement of theme, development of theme, and recapitulation of theme. So, a well-known sonnet such as Shakespeare's Number 73: "That time of year thou mayst in me behold,/When yellow leaves, or none, or few do hang/Upon those boughs which shake against the cold,/Bare ruined choirs, where late the sweet birds sang." certainly opens with a clearly articulated theme. Lines five to twelve then develop or play with that theme, while the couplet recapitulates, restating and clinching the theme in a verbal ralentando, emphasized by using eighteen monosyllables out of nineteen words:

> This thou perceiv'st, which makes thy love more
> strong,
> To love that well, which thou must leave ere long.
> (Dover Wilson 39)

In musical terms, the second part modulates into different keys, so the effect of returning to the dominant, the main key or theme, is one of satisfying resolution. Standard punctuation within such a scheme has a crucial function, pointing the cadences like rests in music, and giving each unit of meaning its appointed place.

In the orbicular sonnet, however, meaning is not spaced out like it is in standard usage, where the links of the syntax prioritize and subordinate, so that everything knows its place. The logic is circular rather than linear, where punctuation becomes a distracting rash on the page rather than an aid to clarity. I have already rather daringly compared Clare's method to Joyce's. I will do so again, reminding you that *Finnegans Wake* dispenses with punctuation in an attempt to elicit from language its depth-charging resonance and simultaneity. If one is foolhardy enough to read the *Wake* through, one finds that it ends in mid-sentence, requiring one to start the book afresh, in mid-sentence. Joyce refuses to sentence us to just one meaning. Similarly, at the end of Clare's sonnets, there is rarely the clinching, epigrammatic, summing-up feeling one gets in the architectural sonnet. At first, this is disorienting, the familiar signposts of the landscape have gone, and the sense of space as distance and of time as linear has gone, too. What we have is a "fluid succession of presents" (Anderson 1), the phrase Joyce used to describe his new method of narration in *A Portrait of the Artist as a Young Man*. In other articles, I have described Clare's vision as cinematic; it is interesting to remember that Joyce founded one of Dublin's first cinemas.

There is also a medieval quality to this vision; a Clare poem is like a *mille fleurs* tapestry that celebrates profusion rather than putting things in their place. Again, a comparison with Joyce is apt, as Joyce once compared his work to the art of medieval manuscripts such as *The Book of Kells*. Clare seems to suspect that punctuation, visual perspective, and power are closely connected. In fact, the landscape gardener Lancelot Brown, who advised landlords to make over their estates on a huge scale, earning the nickname Capability Brown, used to compare his effects to punctuation. He described his methods to Hannah More: "Now *there* I make a comma, and there, where a more decided turn is proper, I make a colon; at another part, where an interruption is desirable to break the view, a parenthesis; now a full stop, and then I begin another subject" (Stroud 201). And the surveyors of enclosure, and later those planning the railways, were busy in Clare's landscape, triangulating it for better efficiency. Furthermore, tourists and artists traveled the countryside with their heads full of the jargon of the Picturesque, "surveying" a landscape from a "station" to find good "prospects", and carrying more instruments in the shape of camera obscuras and Claude glasses. All of these instrumental forces created an environment of massive dis-orientation, dis-placement, and dis-appointment for Clare, eventually driving him mad.

An example of an "orbicular" sonnet is "Emmonsails Heath in Winter":

> I love to see the old heaths withered brake
> Mingle its crimpled leaves with furze & ling
> While the old Heron from the lonely lake
> Starts slow & flaps his melancholly wing
> & oddling crow in idle motions swing
> On the half rotten ash trees topmost twig
> Beside whose trunk the gipsey makes his bed
> Up flies the bouncing wood cock from the brig
> Where a black quagmire quakes beneath the tread
>
> The field fare chatters in the whistling thorn
> & for the awe round fields & closen rove
> & coy bumbarrels twenty in a drove
> Flit down the hedgrows in the frozen plain
> & hang on little twigs & start again
> (Robinson et al. *Middle Period* IV, 286)

No wonder this poem was not published until 1908. Apart from its use of dialect and absence of punctuation, it contains none of the tricks of perspective by which we are accustomed to find our way in most post-Renaissance landscape art. The sonnet, in its unobtrusively skilful way, is a celebration of the kinetic profusion of nature.

In writing like this, Clare performs such a sleight of hand that we can easily overlook the idiosyncratic structure of the poem in our enjoyment of the fleeting impression it gives. Clare himself sometimes helped add to the common impression of his work as artless and untutored in such a statement as: "I used to drop down under a bush and scribble the fresh thoughts on the crown of my hat" (Robinson and Powell, *Clare By Himself,* 100). Clare's later hero, Lord Byron, had a similar throwaway attitude to technique; it is a very Romantic deception.

"Emmonsails Heath in Winter" is very much more than a scribble on the crown of a hat. The cinematic immediacy of the sonnet and the spasmodic and arbitrary movements of the birds in the landscape are paralleled in the rhyme-scheme. The poem, like the heron, "starts slow" with a description of the heath, and with a conventional decasyllabic quatrain, rhymed a, b, a, b. The description of the "oddling crow" begins another syntactical unit, but the "swing" of line five rhymes illogically with "ling" and "wing" of lines two and four of the quatrain, making a tension between the rhyme and the movement of the syntax which keeps the reader's eye alert (another debt to Spenser). Lines six to nine comprise another quatrain, rhyming c, d, c, d, but the "bouncing woodcock" bursts noisily in, making it quite different in effect from the first quatrain, with its melancholy heron. Line ten introduces another incident, this time of two lines, and again one's normal expectations are jolted, as line ten is an "oddling" line, "thorn" not rhyming with any other word. Illogically again, the last four lines of the sonnet are written as two couplets, but their effect is about as different from the clinching effect of the Shakespearean sonnet as it is possible to be. The "bumbarrels" are given a momentary but sharply etched existence, as they flit across one's field of vision, or simply the field, and then they are gone. No comment. No tears. This is just nature performing its mysterious movie-show.

The problems facing an editor or scholar of Clare are manifold. While sympathizing with Jonathan Bate's procedure, in my published scholarship I have endorsed the "primitive" approach. Growing up in Ireland, I became used to literature, even the publication of an inoffensive poem, becoming political. Similarly, a debate has emerged in England about this editorial business, becoming at times acerbic and politicized. For example, the primitive Clare is published by Oxford University Press, as is my 1983 book of literary criticism: *John Clare and Picturesque Landscape*. To my dismay, I am sometimes lumped in with the so-called élitists who are perceived to condescend to Clare by publishing in its naked beauty what he actually wrote. I remain an unrepentant child of the sixties, a decade that did indeed spawn much barbaric nonsense. But I still remember my thrill and astonishment on first reading the 1964 and 1967 raw editions of Clare, edited by Eric Robinson and Geoffrey Summerfield—uncooked, unenclosed, and delicious.

My Oxford book got excellent reviews and sold out, but appeared at a time when European white males (dead or alive), and all their works, were under hostile scrutiny (some of it deserved). In the Age of Theory, Clare's work hardly fared any better than it did in the old class-divided society. The practitioners of the deconstructionist mode largely ignored his work as it seemed, to them, a simplistic language. But a form of deconstruction, it could be argued, is what Clare applied to the conflicting languages of his time. In *The Genius of Shakespeare*, Jonathan Bate argues that the left-wing reaction to the conservative view of Shakespeare, what he calls the New Iconoclasm, is itself limited and partial. In its critique of the conservative view (Shakespeare used as a kind of mascot or figurehead riding on the bonnet of the imperial Rolls-Royce, so to speak), the New Iconoclasm also quotes selectively from the Bard to support its own ideology. Both camps tend to ignore the testimony of millions of readers and play-goers in every corner of the globe who know that, of all writers, Shakespeare goes to the quick of things. "Universal" is a big word, and one perhaps best avoided. Jonathan Swift once made a nice distinction between a human being as an *animal rationale* and as an *animal capax rationis*. (Clifford 116). People, he argued, were all too obviously irrational, but they were capable of rationality. Shakespeare, we might say, is frequently capable of universality.

Clare is not Shakespeare, but I have quoted Bate on Shakespeare because it illustrates that the reputation of some authors fares badly at both ends of the political spectrum. Clare may have been condescendingly referred to for a long time as the "peasant poet," but at least that constituted a form of recognition. Clare's hob-nailed boots may have been out of place in the corridors of Burghley House (where he went to visit the Marquess of Exeter); they are even less likely to scrape the floors of the post-modern Parisian intellectual élite.

Many of Clare's sonnets discuss birds, their nesting habits, their songs, their flight patterns, and their colours. They illustrate what some critics now call his open-field poetics— not free verse, but artful informality. He gives birds, animals, people, even tracts of land, the freedom of his imagination, and is an admirable model for a humane polity that respects the earth. His longer poem "The Nightingale's Nest" reads like an indirect ars poetica, with its patient and humble attention to the bird's artistry. In the following passage, precise ornithology is combined with wistful mythology as the humble but ambitious poet includes a wry self-portrait in his "russet brown" garb:

& her renown
Hath made me marvel that so famed a bird
Should have no better dress than russet brown
Her wings would tremble in her extacy
& feathers stand on end as 't'were with joy
& mouth wide open to release her heart
Of its out sobbing songs
(Robinson et al. *Middle Period* III 457)

All Clare's bird- and bird's-nest poems marvel at this instinctive artistry, which is such a salutary lesson in poetics for the usually self-conscious poet. In the following poem (I quote the first of two sonnet-like stanzas), the form of the English/Shakespearean sonnet (with rhyme scheme varied slightly) lies as a ghostly paradigm behind the writing. Clare also admires the ability of the woodlark to put pursuers off its track by dropping like a stone into its nest, which is described as a "quiet station." He puns on the word station, used, as we saw earlier, in the landscape terminology of his day for the place a tourist, artist, or surveyor stood to get bearings in the landscape in order to visually explore or commercially exploit it. There is also an implied self-reflection as the poet remembers his lowly "station" in society, another link he feels with the bird. Clare lives out Wordsworth's line: "Shine, poet, in thy place and be content":

The wood lark rises from the coppice tree
Time after time untired she upward springs
Silent while up then coming down she sings
A pleasant song of varied melody
Repeated often till some sudden check
The sweet toned impulse of her rapture stops
Then stays her trembling wings & down she drops
Like to a stone amid the crowding kecks

Where underneath some hazels mossy root
Is hid her little low & humble nest
Upon the ground larks love such places best
& here doth well her quiet station suit
As safe as secresy her six eggs lie
Mottled with dusky spots unseen by passers bye
(Robinson et al. *Middle Period* IV, 321-2)

Clare's bird poems are unique in English literature. There is, however, a perhaps surprising parallel in French literature, especially in the verse and prose of some lesser-known writers (outside France) quoted by Gaston Bachelard in his landmark book, *The Poetics of Space* (1958). The following passage by Ambroise Paré echoes Clare's sentiments exactly:

"The enterprise and skill with which animals make their nests is so efficient that it is not possible to do better, so entirely do they surpass all masons, carpenters and builders; for there is not a man who would be able to make a house better suited to himself and to his children than these little animals build for themselves. This is so true, in fact, that we have a proverb according to which men can do everything except build a bird's nest." (92)

And Jules Michelet, described by Bachelard as "one of the greatest dreamers of winged life," writes: "The house is a bird's very person; it is its form and its most immediate effort, I shall even say, its suffering. The result is only obtained by constantly repeated pressure of the breast. There is not one of these blades of grass that, in order to make it curve and hold the curve, has not been pressed on countless times by the bird's breast, its heart." (101). Michelet describes creation as a kind of pain emerging from deprivation: pure Clare.

Here is Clare's prose fragment about the brown linnet: "brown linnet or furze linnet builds in furze bushes on heaths makes a nest of dead grass lined with rabbit fur lays 5 eggs somthing like the former but smaller sprinkled with red and purple spots at the large end" (Robinson and Fitter, *Birds*, 36)

And here is A. Toussenel in *Le Monde des Oiseaux* (1853):

"My recollection of the first bird's nest that I found all by myself has remained more deeply engraved on my memory than that of the first prize I won in grammar school for a Latin version. It was a lovely linnet's nest with four pinkish-gray eggs striated with red lines, like an emblematical map. I was seized with an emotion of such indescribable delight that I stood there for over an hour, glued to one spot, looking. That day, by chance, I found my vocation." (Bachelard 95)

There is a Zen quality to Clare's vocation. In the words of Lao Tzu:

"Knead clay in order to make a vessel. Adapt the nothing therein to the purpose in hand, and you will have the use of the vessel. Cut out doors and windows in order to make a room. Adapt the nothing therein to the purpose in hand, and you will have the use of the room." (Lau 67)

Clare knows that birds' nests are never empty, even when deserted. He always adapts the nothing therein to the purpose in hand. The innermost places of nature are full of the abundance of our alienation. Instead of avoiding the void, Clare embraces it, and gives it a voice unlike any other.

19

LATE EXPECTATIONS

One of the reasons I like Thomas Hardy's poetry so much is that he came to it late in his career—at the age of fifty-eight. He was already a famous novelist and a trained architect. There is a freedom in his poetry as if he were saying to himself: "I can write what I like now. It doesn't have to fit any particular mould or fashion." To this day, it remains unfashionable.

Hardy made up for lost time; the Macmillan edition of the *Complete Poems* (1976) prints nine hundred and forty-seven poems. This is a huge output for a lyric poet—other writers such as Hopkins and Larkin, for example, have made major reputations with a relatively slender output. Emily Dickinson must hold the lyric marathon record, with over nineteen hundred poems completed; in spite of this, she remains a minimalist—give her a mile and she'll take an inch.

Hardy's self-scrutiny is arresting and slightly comic, caught in poem 509 in an almost illicit act of composition:

> I looked up from my writing,
> And gave a start to see,

As if rapt in my inditing,
The moon's full gaze on me.

Her meditative misty head
Was spectral in its air,
And I involuntarily said,
"What are you doing there?"

"Oh, I've been scanning pond and hole
And waterway hereabout
For the body of one with a sunken soul
Who has put his life-light out.

"Did you hear his frenzied tattle?
It was sorrow for his son
Who is slain in brutish battle,
Though he has injured none.

"And now I am curious to look
Into the blinkered mind
Of one who wants to write a book
In a world of such a kind."

Her temper overwrought me,
And I edged to shun her view,
For I felt assured she thought me
One who should drown him too.
(Gibson 551)

Every poet must have felt the emotion that is the ostensible
subject of this poem: why am I sitting here scribbling in a
universe of so much pain and injustice? Eliot asked a similar
question as he worked on the *Four Quartets* during the Blitz;
Yeats felt a pang of envy as he talked to a soldier during the

240

Irish Civil War. This guilt, if that is what to call it, has called forth some of the greatest prose in the language: Sidney's *Apologie for Poetry*, Milton's prose, Shelley's *Defense of Poetry*, Wordsworth's Preface to *Lyrical Ballads*, Yeats's *Autobiographies*, T. S. Eliot's and Heaney's essays. These are polemics in the best sense, reasoned counter-arguments to the busybodies of this world. Sidney was replying to a particularly virulent pamphlet, full of the puritan mistrust and denigration of poetry.

But deep down, these poets know that the argument is pointless. The musician who composed "Greensleeves" was no doubt neglecting his or her immediate social duties, but because music is perceived as a universal art, musicians are rarely called upon to write apologies for music. Hardy, who was a great ironist, here has the last laugh, because the verbal music of this poem is so assured and haunting that it is likely to stick in the craw of even the most conscientious objector.

The main argument given here is a lunar one; if the poet pays it too much heed, he is in danger of becoming a lunatic and of searching out the nearest pond. Hardy, by implication, is asserting a solar, Apollonian counter-argument—in spite of life's tragedies, it is reasonable to keep going, and, since writing is what writers do, to keep writing. But it is necessarily writing in a minor key, an equivalent of Virgil's *"Sunt lacrimae rerum et mentem mortalia tangunt"* ("These are the tears of things and mortal things cut our hearts to the quick.")

It is Hardy's plangent verbal music that subtly cuts our hearts and echoes in our inner ears. Unfortunately, some teachers of literature have not developed discriminating in-

241

ner ears, and in any case rarely read aloud to their students, so a poem such as this is not likely to cut much ice in academe. But Hardy was not writing for academe, he was writing for anyone with ears to hear and hearts to feel. He seems to say: whenever you feel suicidal, take this poem and recite it, mouth it, whisper it, shout it—anything but over-intellectualize it. You are in the school of life, not doing a Ph. D. in Hardy's use of lunar imagery.

Another poem ideal for reciting, mouthing, whispering is "On One Who Lived and Died Where He Was Born," number 621 in the *Complete Poems*. Again, this is the kind of poem unlikely to be mentioned, let alone analyzed, in a graduate seminar. It belongs to that species of neglected, old-fashioned, endearing works, the equivalent of maiden aunts in the nineteenth century quietly knitting in the corner; everyone was fond of such creatures but would never think of asking their views on anything. That gives such a work a kind of virginal immunity from fashion and ideology, the opposite of some anthology chestnuts eyeballed and discussed to the point of distortion, an attrition analogous to the defacement of a stone head on the side of a cathedral by centuries of rain. A large number of Hardy's poems belong to this demure sorority:

> When a night in November
> Blew forth its bleared airs
> An infant descended
> His birth-chamber stairs
> For the very first time,
> At the still, midnight chime;
> All unapprehended
> His mission, his aim.—
> Thus, first, one November,

242

An infant descended
The stairs.

On a night in November
Of weariful cares,
A frail aged figure
Ascended those stairs
For the very last time:
All gone his life's prime,
All vanished his vigour,
And fine, forceful frame:
Thus, last, one November
Ascended that figure
Upstairs.

On those nights in November—
Apart eighty years—
The babe and the bent one
Who traversed those stairs
From the early first time
To the last feeble climb—
That fresh and that spent one—
Were even the same:
Yea, who passed in November
As infant, as bent one,
Those stairs.

Wise child of November!
From birth to blanched hairs
Descending, ascending,
Wealth-wantless, those stairs;
Who saw quick in time
As a vain pantomime
Life's tending, its ending,

The worth of its fame.
Wise child of November,
Descending, ascending
Those stairs!
(Gibson 659-60)

The gait of this poem, with its awkward inversions and archaic diction, is that of a countryman—not maybe "the forced gait of a shuffling nag" but close. For all its felicitousness of technique, it resists the kind of polish a master such as Yeats would give it. Where Yeats tends to strut, Hardy stumbles—if the former is sometimes a bit superhuman, the latter is endearing in the double sense that Hopkins uses so touchingly in "Felix Randal": "This seeing the sick endears them to us, us too it endears." (Gardner 48). This tenderness is reminiscent of many moments in the work of that other countryman, Shakespeare.

Two modern poets, Philip Larkin and Seamus Heaney, have both testified to their great admiration for Yeats's work, while admitting also a deep affection for Hardy's. Of the two, Hardy seems to have been a more lasting begetter of verbal progeny in Larkin and Heaney, among other poets. Larkin's deliberate bleakness is often softened by a Hardyesque charity, an influence operating rather like that famous arrow-shower at the end of "The Whitsun Weddings"—"somewhere becoming rain" (Thwaite 94). And in Heaney, especially his later work, a fully achieved poet can simultaneously allude to past literature and to his own earlier work, knowing that it, too, is part of our mental furniture. In the exquisite "The Blackbird of Glanmore" from his most recent volume, *District and Circle*, Heaney writes: "Hedge-hop, I am absolute/For you " (76), with its allusion to "Be absolute for death . . ." in *Measure for Measure*. He also harks back to an early poem,

"Mid-term Break", about the loss of his brother, killed by a car at the age of four, and here the Hardy influence falls like a soft drizzle of tenderness:

> And I think of one gone to him,
> A little stillness dancer—
> Haunter-son, lost brother—
> Cavorting through the yard,
> So glad to see me home,
>
> My homesick first term over.
> (75)

That lost brother has been descending, ascending the stairs of the poet's memory in an arrested dance of death all this time.

If Hardy has moments of tenderness, he is better known for his bleakness, his determination to take the shine off our bliss. And, of course, Shakespeare's moments of tenderness are like asides, stills, lay-byes in the course of a generally dire onrushing momentum. Both Shakespeare and Hardy had taken the measure of nature and human life and found both irretrievably flawed. On his eighty-sixth birthday, Hardy wrote a poem called "He Never Expected Much," (Gibson 873) which we can take with a large pinch of salt, rather like we do when Yeats in his epitaph instructs us to "Cast a cold eye"; Yeats was incapable of assessing anything with a cold eye. Such a passionate man as Hardy must have expected multitudes. Both Yeats and Hardy are Geminis, and are here calling upon their other more chilled-out twins. Hardy's twin convinces him that the world had provided "Just neutral-tinted haps," which represents either Hardy in his dotage or the famous irony again:

HE NEVER EXPECTED MUCH
[or]
A Consideration
[A reflection] on My Eighty-Sixth Birthday

Well, World, you have kept faith with me,
Kept faith with me;
Upon the whole you have proved to be
Much as you said you were.
Since as a child I used to lie
Upon the leaze and watch the sky,
Never, I own, expected I
That life would all be fair.

'Twas then you said, and since have said,
Times since have said,
In that mysterious voice you shed
From hills and clouds around:
"Many have loved me desperately,
Many with smooth serenity,
While some have shown contempt of me
Till they dropped underground.

I do not promise overmuch,
Child, overmuch;
Just neutral-tinted haps and such,"
You said to minds like mine.
Wise warning for your credit's sake!
Which I for one failed not to take,
And hence could stem such strain and ache
As each year might assign.
(Gibson 886)

Readers of Hardy's novels, with their moral earthquakes,

will chuckle at the eleventh-hour serenity of this poem. They know that, in his poetry and his prose, rarely have such musical strains been wrought from such profound, and far from neutral, aches.

20

A TASTE OF IRELAND

Sicily, 1961. I was twenty, on my way to stay with a school friend in Malta. I had a few hours to kill in the port of Syracuse before the ferry left, so I entered a small, dark café and, not having much spare cash, ordered a peach. It arrived, the largest peach I have ever seen, on an equally ample plate. I cut it into slices and embarked on a veritable assault course on my taste-buds. For someone used to the rigours of a more northerly culinary clime (and one recently released from boarding schools where overcooked turnips constituted a feast), that simple meal was a revelation. The peach permeated my whole body with delight—it truly was "a beaker full of the warm south." It was an education in the generous physicality of the Mediterranean world, a sensuousness that seemed age-old and wise. This feeling is expressed in Rilke's *Sonnets to Orpheus* (number 13):

> Ripe apple, pear and banana,
> gooseberry . . . They speak of life and death
> as soon as they get in our mouths . . .
> Try watching a child's face: you can
>
> see the far-off knowledge as he tastes it. (Young 27)

A friend once commented as I relished an Italian meal: "It is a sin to enjoy your food." If that is so, I have been doomed all my life.

I was not alone in this physical and spiritual hunger for a more stimulating culinary world. Up to about 1960 in Ireland, for example, olive oil was mostly regarded as a medicine, bought in tiny bottles in the chemist; garlic was off-limits because it was regarded as antisocial. Knowledge of herbs was scanty, and as for edible flowers: are you crazy? Terence Conran has written recently, in the introduction to a reissue of Elizabeth David's book, *Italian Food*, first published in 1954:

"Elizabeth David changed the UK. In the early fifties, when much of the British Isles was grey, broken, and rationed, her books brought the hope of a different sort of sunny, colourful, well-fed life. As we toured the small market towns of France and Italy, we thought: Why should we not have this food, colour, and charm in our own lives? Why shouldn't we have markets filled with a profusion of vegetables, fruit, fish, meat, poultry, spices and good humour like they do? Why shouldn't we drink wine and sit outdoors on café terraces?" (ix)

My childhood memories of food are of Southern Ireland in the 1940s and 1950s. As always, there were Irish differences that need explaining. First, the Republic of Ireland had remained neutral in the Second World War (although many Irish men and women served in the forces). Ireland was more fortunate than the Britain that Conran describes; not only had Ireland avoided extensive bomb damage, but wholesome food was more available at all levels of society. Although wartime supplies were scarce (tea was one pound for a pound), rationing lifted earlier than in the UK, and Ireland had rich supplies of fresh ingredients—cream, butter, beef, and pork were plentiful. Hughes Brothers made their delicious ice creams with milk; the English Wall's ice cream was made with pig fat. Second, Ireland had never had an Industrial Revolution, so the small-scale rural networks remained, similar to those still existing in provincial France and Italy. Third, Ireland was always culturally a few decades or more behind the "progress" of other major European countries; the Ireland I remember was really a late Victorian/Edwardian society in many respects. Practices and niceties that in England had already become "quaint" were part of life, such as grace before meals. My mother used to sieve coarse flour through silk stockings. People lived closer to the rhythms and realities of nature: bloody carcases adorned butchers' shops; if you asked for kidneys, they were cut out in front of you. Much food was available only in season, giving it extra relish.

Ireland was then an economically poor country, but rich in human and natural resources. The resilience of people who, by today's standards, had very little in the way of material goods, was remarkable. In his heart-warming book, *It's a Long Way from Penny Apples*, Bill Cullen describes how, with careful thrift and heroic efforts on the part of the womenfolk, even inhabitants of overcrowded inner-city areas could get by:

"There was nothing like an evening meal of crispy turf-fire-grilled Howth herrings or mackerel. A sprinkling of vinegar. Potatoes roasted in the fire. The Ma would make some white lemon sauce for the Da, and the kids would get a dip. Lots of small, easily chewed bones in the herrings. "Lots of calcium to help your growth," Mother Darcy said. Between the apples and bananas, the vegetable stews and the fish, the inner-city youngsters had a meat-free, healthy diet growing up."

Howth is still a fishing port, with prosperous fish shops along the quay. As children living near Howth, we caught mackerel on the way to picnics on Ireland's Eye from our little seventeen-foot "Mermaid." Like the Cullen family, we were great eaters of vegetables. I remember driving in the side gate of Howth Castle, the local demesne, to buy vegetables in the stable yard. I have never since seen cabbages like that—they squeaked when you touched them, they were so green and waxy.

It is hard to imagine, even for people who experienced them, just how easy-going, slow-paced and personalized, things were then. The Howth tram circled the Hill of Howth at ten miles an hour, the open top giving spectacular views of Dublin Bay. A regular sight on the tram was Mrs. Forman, with her basket of fish and seafood. She once gave my sister a live lobster on hearing it was her birthday. The Formans had been in Howth since Viking times, predating by several centuries the Norman Gaisford St. Lawrences of Howth Castle. As our housekeeper, Nan Carrick, used to say: "There was a Carrick in Sutton before there was a Lord in Howth."

Milk was delivered to our gate by Peter Moore, the milkman, with his horse and cart, and ladled out of big milk churns. The horse would saunter on to the next customer's gate and wait for Peter to catch up. The Johnston, Mooney and O'Brien bread van delivered the bread, the driver having to shovel out a loaf from the deeps of the trays as Nan haggled with him over choice and price. Nan had a sharp eye for cuts of meat as well, and a visit to Finnegan's at Sutton

Cross could take twenty minutes: "Do you call those chops? Don't give me that terrible tack." My mother left such everyday shopping to Nan, who, although scrupulously honest, managed to supply some of her hard-up neighbours out of my mother's budget. My brother later met a lad in Howth village who plied him with drink and told him that our family had unwittingly kept his family going for years.

Many of the Dublin shops were venerable family firms, such as Findlaters, who owned twenty-six shops located all over Dublin. The attendants greeted every customer by name, knowing their preferences. I had a strange habit of putting marmalade on sausages, the clear "Little Chip" marmalade supplied by Leverett and Frye of Grafton Street. These shops, and others like them, had a fleet of messenger bicycles, sturdy vehicles with a small front wheel surmounted by a capacious basket. Deliveries were made every day, often to far-flung customers. Alex Findlater recently showed me a huge vault on his business premises, crammed with old messenger bicycles. In 1982, Alex rode one of these bikes in a Bloomsday re-enactment of passages in Joyce, handing pork chops to the Lord Mayor in his coach. Alex inaugurated a Bloomsday bike rally, still going strong, which has raised over half a million pounds for Dublin children.

The best food in Dublin in the fifties, if you could afford it, was in the Russell Hotel. The chef's main advice to pupils was: "If a dish doesn't come out right, keep adding butter and cream." The best place for afternoon tea was the Shelbourne Hotel (it still is, having just had an eighty-three million euro makeover). On a more homely level, the nearby Country Shop made wonderful potato cakes, served beside open smoky turf fires. The best seafood was in the Redbank on D'Olier Street, famous for Dublin Bay prawns, the best cocktails in the Buttery of the Hibernian Hotel. The best steaks were in the Dolphin, as well as the Unicorn on Merrion Row, given its name by Sheela Coffey, whose husband was a distinguished Irish scholar. The rent remained low, as the building had acquired a dubious reputation ever since W. B. Yeats and his friends had held séances there. The best beef could be bought in Buckley's of Moore Street, the best coffee and blended teas in Bewley's of Grafton Street. The jewel of Dublin dining in the post-war years was Jammet's restaurant on the corner of Grafton and Nassau Streets. English people with a taste for good living escaped the austerities of rationed Britain, loving the understated elegance of the place. John Betjeman lived in Ireland during the forties, and Evelyn Waugh was a regular visitor, writing in his diary: "I think that I have never been so much attracted by any restaurant as by Jammet's."

The rural equivalent of Jammet's was, and is, Hunter's Hotel, a family-run hotel near Ashford, County Wicklow. The travel writer, Jan Morris, pays an annual visit, and extols its tranquillity, friendliness, lush gardens, cosy bar with old photographs, and eschewal of fashion: the light fittings in the dining-room are pure country Ireland, circa 1949. The food, however, is contemporary and very good. On a recent visit, I chose a completely Irish menu: smoked wild Irish salmon with brown bread, Wicklow lamb from a few miles away, and a selection of Irish cheeses. As I looked out the window from my table, I saw a sign that sums up the old-world charm of Hunter's: "Ladies and gentlemen will not, and others must not, pull the flowers in this garden."

There was a time, unbelievably, when I hated cheese—but I was thinking of those slabs of dark yellow Irish Cheddar ubiquitous at that time. It was during a childhood holiday in Switzerland that cheese took on a different meaning (a revelation analogous to my epiphany in Sicily). I started to collect the colourful labels (the big round one on the outside, the little triangular ones inside) of Swiss and French cheeses. Irish cheese making had a remarkable revival after 1973, when EEC regulations created a milk surplus. Irish cheeses are now abundant, and rejoice in names such as Gubbeens, Gigginstown, Laviston, and Mulleen.

The Irish Elizabeth David is Myrtle Allen of Ballymaloe House, County Cork. Myrtle and her husband have been in the forefront of the locally bought, fresh-food revolution. In 1996, my wife and I were having lunch at Ballymaloe; at the next table were Martha Stewart and her entourage. After a light lunch, they took off from the front lawn in a helicopter, presumably thinking they had "done" County Cork. Nothing could be further from the spirit of Ballymaloe than such a whirlwind visit. It is a deeply peaceful place; everything is done in impeccable taste, far from the designer look. Like many of the best Irish hotels and restaurants, it feels like the family home it is.

The ingredients in this part of Ireland are superb—thick cream, huge strawberries, succulent beef. As well as having had the gall to open an Irish restaurant in Paris, the Allens stress the Irish/French wine connection. Half a dozen Bordeaux vineyards were founded or are still part-owned by Irish families: Lynch-Bages and Château Kirwan are examples. The Bartons of Barton-Guestier are from County Meath, and the Hennessy family founded the famous brandy. For centuries, the favourite wine in Ireland was claret, as in eighteenth-century England. There is a continental feel to this part of Ireland: from Waterford to Baltimore on the southernmost tip of County Cork, the coast faces France. There is a lookout tower above Baltimore Harbour; locals say as you walk in that direction: "Are you going to Spain?"

I began these reminiscences with an expansion of the senses, implying that all Irish food in those days was dull, the meat-and-three-veg. style. As the joke goes: "Are you having gravy; one lump or two?" But many households, my mother's included, ate well within the limits I have described. The main events in my mother's culinary year were Christmas and Easter, preparations starting months in advance. Mrs. Ramsay in Virginia Woolf's *To the Lighthouse*, creating a fleeting work of art in the details of her dinner party, could be a portrait of my mother. And, years later, when I read *Monet's Table* by Claire Joyes, I recognised the same sense of food as an honoured family ritual, the handsome place settings, the flowers specially chosen, the ensemble subtly visualised; nothing overdone, everything lovingly particularized. The following is a recreation of my mother's Easter lunch, April 1955. In 1953, we had moved from Howth to a farm near Avoca, County Wicklow, in the "Garden of Ireland." Our farm supplied milk and cream, vegetables, herbs, grapes, and flowers. Meat was bought from Sharpe's in Avoca (the Ballykissangel of television fame), who delivered by bicycle. Trips to Dublin provided smoked salmon from Sawyers of Chatham Street, and coffee from Bewley's. A dry sherry beforehand, an inexpensive claret, a jug of iced water, and perhaps a brandy or port with the cheese, completed this unsophisticated but deeply satisfying feast:

Smoked Atlantic salmon
Lemon slices
Red pepper
Irish soda bread

255

Roast Wicklow lamb
Home-made mint sauce
Home-made redcurrant jelly
Early fresh peas
Early broad or runner beans
New potatoes, buttered and parsleyed

Rhubarb tart with home-made pastry
Cream (lashings of)

Camembert
Biscuits

Coffee
Cream

Milk-chocolate Easter eggs

The following recipes were traditionally, but not exclusively, used at Hallowe'en. October 31st was called All Hallows Eve and November 1st All Saints' Day. Charms (a sixpence, a button, an ornament) were wrapped up and put in the Colcannon. My mother had a collection of tiny silver charms, which were a delight to unwrap.

COLCANNON

One lb. kale or cabbage
One lb. potatoes
Six spring onions
Five fluid ounces of milk or cream
Salt and pepper
Four ounces of butter, melted

Shred the kale or cabbage leaves and cook them until tender. Cook the potatoes in their skins; drain, peel potatoes. Mash them until smooth.

Simmer onions in milk or cream for five minutes. Add this liquid to potatoes; beat well. Beat in the kale or cabbage; add salt and pepper. Heat over a gentle heat; serve with a well in the centre for the melted butter.

TEA BRACK

This is a variant of *BAIRM BRACK* (speckled yeast loaf in Gaelic), the bread eaten traditionally at Hallowe'en. It is best served in very thin slices, lightly buttered, accompanied by strong tea.

Eight ounces sultanas
Eight ounces raisins
Two ounces orange and lemon zest
Eight ounces dark brown sugar
Sixteen fluid ounces strong black tea
Twelve ounces plain flour
Two teaspoons baking powder
Two teaspoons mixed spice
Two eggs, beaten
Two tablespoons liquid honey, for glaze

Line a cake tin with greaseproof paper and grease with butter.

Put sultanas, raisins, peel and sugar in a large bowl and pour the hot tea into the bowl. Stir. Soak overnight.

Sieve together the flour, baking powder and spice. Mix the

beaten eggs and the flour into the fruit mixture, beating well.

Pour into cake tin, and bake for one-and-a-half hours. Ten minutes before end of cooking time, heat the honey and brush onto the cake. Return to oven for ten minutes.

LIST OF PRINCIPAL SOURCES

Abrams, M.H. et al. eds. *The Norton Anthology of English Literature*, Sixth Edition, Vol. I. New York: W.W. Norton, 2003.

_____. *The Norton Anthology of English Literature*, Sixth Edition, Vol, 2. New York: W.W. Norton, 1993.

Anderson, Chester G. ed. *James Joyce: A Portrait of the Artist as a Young Man.* Harmondsworth: Penguin, 1968.

Attridge, Derek, ed. *The Cambridge Companion to James Joyce.* Cambridge: Cambridge University Press, 1990.

Bachelard, Gaston. *The Poetics of Space.* Boston: Beacon Press, 1994.

Bate, Jonathan. *The Genius of Shakespeare.* London: Picador, 1997.

Bloom, Harold and Lionel Trilling, eds. *Romantic Poetry and Prose.* London: Oxford University Press, 1973.

Blunt, Wilfrid. *The Compleat Naturalist: The Life of Linnaeus.* New York: Viking Press, 1971.

Brewer, John. *The Pleasures of the Imagination: English Culture in the Eighteenth Century.* New York: Farrar, Straus and Giroux, 1997.

Brownlow, Timothy. *Climbing Croagh Patrick.* Lantzville, B.C.: Oolichan Books, 1998.

Bryson, Bill. *Notes from a Small Island.* Toronto: McClelland & Stewart, 1998.

Clark, Kenneth. *The Nude.* Harmondsworth: Penguin, 1960.

_____. *Civilisation*. London: British Broadcasting Corporation and John Murray, 1970.

Clifford, James L. ed. *Eighteenth-Century English Literature*. New York: Oxford University Press, 1959.

Cruise O'Brien, Conor. *The Great Melody: A Thematic Biography of Edmund Burke*. Chicago: University of Chicago Press, 1993.

Donoghue, Denis. *The Integrity of Yeats*. Cork: The Mercier Press, 1964.

Dover Wilson, John, ed. *Shakespeare: The Sonnets*. Cambridge: Cambridge University Press, 1969.

Dunn, Susan, ed. *Jean-Jacques Rousseau: The Social Contract and The First and Second Discourses*. New Haven: Yale University Press, 2002.

Finneran, Richard J. ed. *The Collected Poems of W. B. Yeats*. New York: Simon & Schuster, 1996.

Fleeman, J.D., ed. *Boswell: Life of Johnson*. London: Oxford University Press, 1970.

Foster, R. F. *W. B. Yeats: A Life. Vol. I*. Oxford: Oxford University Press, 1998.

Frost, Robert. *A Witness Tree*. New York: Henry Holt, 1942.

_____. *A Further Range: Book Six*. New York: Henry Holt, 1936.

Frye, Northrop, ed. *Romanticism Reconsidered*. New York: Columbia University Press, 1963.

Gardner, W. H. ed. *Poems and Prose of Gerard Manley Hopkins*. Harmondsworth: Penguin, 1968.

Geddes, Gary, ed. *20th-Century Poetry & Poetics.* Toronto: Oxford University Press, 1996.

Gibson, James, ed. *Thomas Hardy: The Complete Poems.* London: Macmillan, 1981.

Gill, Stephen, ed. *William Wordsworth: The Major Works.* Oxford: Oxford University Press, 2000.

Gittings, Robert. *John Keats.* Harmondsworth: Penguin, 1971.

_____, ed. *Letters of John Keats.* London: Oxford University Press, 1970.

Goodridge, John, ed. *The John Clare Society Journal.* No. 13, July 1994; No. 14, July 1995.

Guest, John, ed. *The Best of Betjeman.* Harmondsworth: Penguin, 1978.

Harrington, John P. ed. *Modern Irish Drama.* New York: W. W. Norton, 1991.

Harrison, G. B. ed. *The Tragedy of King Lear.* Harmondsworth: Penguin, 1961.

Heaney, Seamus. *Finders Keepers.* New York: Farrar, Straus, Giroux, 2002.

_____. *Seeing Things.* London: Faber and Faber, 1991.

_____. *New Selected Poems* 1966-1987. London: Faber and Faber, 1990.

_____. *District and Circle.* London: Faber and Faber, 2006.

_____. *The Redress of Poetry: Oxford Lectures*. London: Faber and Faber, 1995.

Holden, Anthony. *Olivier*. Harmondsworth: Penguin, 1989.

Hunt, John Dixon and Peter Willis, eds. *The Genius of the Place: The English Landscape Garden 1620-1820*. London: Paul Elek, 1975.

Ignatieff, Michael. *Isaiah Berlin: A Life*. Harmondsworth: Penguin Books, 2000.

Jacobus, Lee A., ed. *A World of Ideas: Essential Readings for College Writers*. Boston: Bedford/St. Martin's, 2002.

James, C.L.R. *Beyond a Boundary*. London: Yellow Jersey Press, 2005.

Jeffares, A. Norman. *W. B. Yeats: A New Biography*. London: Arrow Books, 1990.

Jung, C. G. *Memories, Dreams, Reflections*. London: Collins, 1963.

Kavanagh, Patrick. *Collected Poems*. New York: W.W. Norton, 1973.

Kermode, Frank, ed. *The Tempest*. London: Methuen, 1962.

Lathem, Edward Connery, ed. *The Poetry of Robert Frost*. New York: Henry Holt, 1969.

Lau, D.C. *Lao Tzu: Tao Te Ching*. Harmondsworth: Penguin, 1963.

Lewis, Gifford. *Somerville and Ross: The World of the Irish R. M.* Harmondsworth: Penguin, 1985.

Longley, Michael. *Collected Poems*. London: Jonathan Cape, 2006.

Oliver, Mary. *Rules for the Dance*. Boston: Houghton Mifflin, 1998.

McDiarmid, Lucy and Maureen Waters, eds. *Lady Gregory: Selected Writings*. Harmondsworth: Penguin Books, 1995.

McGann, Jerome J., ed. *Lord Byron: The Major Works*. Oxford: Oxford University Press, 2000.

Milosz, Czeslaw. *The Collected Poems*. New Jersey: Ecco Press, 1988.

Moore, George. *Ave*. London: Heinemann, 1947.

Paglia, Camille. *Sexual Personae*. New York: Random House, 1991.

——————————. *Break, Blow, Burn*. New York: Random House, 2005.

Perkins, David. "How the Romantics Recited Poetry." *Studies in English Literature, 31* (1991).

——————————, ed. *English Romantic Writers*. San Diego: Harcourt Brace Jovanovich, 1967.

Pevsner, Nikolaus. *The Englishness of English Art*. Harmondsworth: Penguin, 1964.

Rees, Richard, trans. *Simone Weil: Selected Essays 1934-43*. London: Oxford University Press, 1963.

Rieu, E. V. trans. *Homer: The Odyssey*. Harmondsworth: Penguin, 1991.

Robinson, F. N. ed. *The Works of Geoffrey Chaucer*. London: Oxford University Press, 1957.

Robinson, Eric and David Powell, eds. *John Clare by Himself*. Ashington, Northumberland: The Mid Northumberland Arts Group and Carcanet Press, 1996.

Robinson, Eric, David Powell and P. M. S. Dawson, eds. *John Clare: Poems of the Middle Period 1822-1837. Vols. I, II, III, IV*. Oxford: Clarendon Press, 1996.

Robinson, Eric and Richard Fitter, eds. *John Clare's Birds*. Oxford: Oxford University Press, 1982.

Rosenthal, M.L. *Running to Paradise: Yeats's Poetic Art*. New York: Oxford University Press, 1994.

Rousseau, Jean-Jacques. *The Confessions*. Harmondsworth: Penguin Books, 1973.

Saddlemyer, Ann, ed. *The Playboy of the Western World and Other Plays*. Oxford: Oxford University Press, 1995.

Sassoon, Siegfried. *Selected Poems*. London: Faber and Faber, 1970.

Schama, Simon. *Landscape and Memory*. Toronto: Random House, 1996.

_____. *Citizens: A Chronicle of the French Revolution*. New York: Random House, 1989.

Scholes, Robert and A. Walton Litz, eds. *James Joyce: Dubliners*. Harmondsworth: Penguin, 1996.

Sinclair, John D. trans. *Dante's Paradiso*. New York: Oxford University Press, 1961.

Stallworthy, Jon. *Between the Lines: Yeats's Poetry in the Making.* Oxford: Clarendon Press, 1963.

Storey, Mark, ed. *John Clare: Selected Letters.* Oxford: Oxford University Press, 1990.

Stroud, Dorothy. *Capability Brown.* London: Faber and Faber, 1975.

Thomas, Edward. *The Collected Poems of Edward Thomas.* Oxford: Oxford University Press, 1981.

Thomas, Keith. *Man and the Natural World: Changing Attitudes in England 1500-1800.* Harmondsworth: Penguin, 1984.

Thomas, R.S. *Selected Poems* 1946-1968. Bloodaxe Books, 1986.

Thwaite, Anthony, ed. *Philip Larkin: Collected Poems.* New York: Farrar, Straus and Giroux, 2003.

Tillyard, Stella. *Aristocrats.* London: Random House, 1995.

Wells, Stanley and Gary Taylor et al, eds. *Shakespeare: Classical Plays.* London: The Folio Society, 1997.

_____. *Shakespeare: Tragedies.* London: The Folio Society, 1997.

_____. *Shakespeare: Early Comedies.* London: The Folio Society, 1997.

_____. *Shakespeare: Tragicomedies.* London: The Folio Society, 1997.

Woolf, Virginia. *To the Lighthouse.* Oxford: Oxford University Press, 1992.

_____. *Mrs. Dalloway*. Harmondsworth: Penguin, 1964.

Wordsworth, Jonathan, M.H. Abrams, Stephen Gill, eds. *William Wordsworth: The Prelude, 1799, 1805, 1850*. New York: W. W. Norton, 1979.

Wu, Duncan, ed. *Romanticism: An Anthology*. Oxford: Blackwell, 2006.

Yeats, W. B. *Essays and Introductions*. London: Macmillan, 1961.

_____. *Autobiographies*. London: Macmillan, 1961.

Young, David, trans. *Rainer Maria Rilke: Sonnets to Orpheus*. New Hampshire: University Press of New England, 1987.

ACKNOWLEDGEMENTS

"Only Connect" was originally published electronically on the University of Maryland's Romantic Circles Website at http://www.rc.umd.edu/pedagogies/commons/ecology.

"A Taste of Ireland" first appeared in *Apples under the Bed: Recollections and Recipes from B.C. Writers and Artists*, ed. Joan Coldwell (Hedgerow Press, 2007).

"Curriculum for Bards" first appeared in a slightly different version as "A Bard's Curriculum" in the *Humanist in Canada* (now *Humanist Perspectives*), Vol. 36, No. 147, Winter, 2004.

"The Loneliness of the Long-Distance Writer" first appeared in *The Art Tree*, ed. Allan Brown (Far Field Press, 2001).

Selections from "Random Thoughts about Literature and Teaching" were first published in *The Fair Exchange*, the journal of the Vancouver Island University (formerly Malaspina University-College) Faculty Association, Issue 11, November 26, 2004.

Some paragraphs from "Fieldwork" originally appeared in *The John Clare Society Journal*, ed, Pauline Buttery. No. 3, July 1984.

"And Joy the Art of True Believing" was delivered at a joint conference of the James Hogg and John Clare Societies at Saint Catherine's College, Oxford, 2001.

"Fairies and Ferries" was delivered as an invited lecture to the Department of Liberal Studies, Vancouver Island University (formerly Malaspina University-College), 2005.

"Fieldwork" was delivered as part of a visiting workshop for a course on "The History of the Sonnet," Vancouver Island University (formerly Malaspina University-College), 2005.

"The Weight of Too Much Liberty" was delivered at one of the launches of *In Fine Form: the Canadian Book of Form Poetry* (Raincoast Books, 2005).

The poem that concludes "The Weight of Too Much Liberty" was first published in *Hermathena*, 1972; it also appeared in *Climbing Croagh Patrick* (Oolichan Books, 1998).

"The Singing-Masters of my Soul" was delivered as the inaugural lecture in the series "Poets on Campus" at Vancouver Island University (formerly Malaspina University-College), 2006.

"Rousseau: Taking the Rough with the Smooth" was delivered as part of a series—"Dangerous Ideas in History"—in the Department of Liberal Studies, Vancouver Island University (formerly Malaspina University-College), 2007.

"Poetry for Supper" by R. S. Thomas is quoted in full with the permission of Bloodaxe Books, Highgreen, Tarset, Northumberland, NE 48 1RP, UK.

"The Silken Tent" and "The Master Speed" from *The Poetry of Robert Frost* edited by Edward Connery Lathem. Copyright 1969 by Henry Holt and Company. Copyright 1936, 1942 by Robert Frost, copyright 1964, 1970 by Lesley Frost

Ballantine. Reprinted by permission of Henry Holt and Company, LLC.

My grateful thanks go to Ron Smith, whose stringent insights have generated much new material.

My thanks to Hiro Boga, who has efficiently supervised the editing of the text.

Michael Warren has given incisive feedback and advice.

And thanks to my wife, Jennifer, for her sweet attention.

Author photo: Geoffrey Jamieson

Tim Brownlow was born in Dublin, Ireland. He was co-editor of a major Irish literary journal before coming to Canada in 1970. After teaching at several universities in Nova Scotia, he came to B. C. in 1991, taking up a position at Malaspina University-College in 1992, from which he retired in 2006. He is now an Honorary Research Associate of the college. As well as scholarly publications, he has published three volumes of verse; the most recent, *Climbing Croagh Patrick* (Oolichan, 1998), was praised by W. J. Keith for its "civilised sincerity." His work appears in a number of anthologies, both scholarly and literary, including *The Penguin Book of Irish Verse*; *The Critical Perspective* (Chelsea House, New York); *Poems for Clare* (UK); *In Fine Form: The Canadian Book of Form Poetry* (Raincoast Books); and *Apples Under the Bed* (Hedgerow Press). His work is featured in the June 2007 edition of *Poetry Ireland Review*.